CAMPAIGN 302

THE THAMES 1813

The War of 1812 on the Northwest Frontier

JOHN F. WINKLER

ILLUSTRATED BY PETER DENNIS
Series editor Marcus Cowper

First published in Great Britain in 2016 by Osprey Publishing,
PO Box 883, Oxford, OX1 9PL, UK
1385 Broadway, 5th Floor, New York, NY 10018, USA
E-mail: info@ospreypublishing.com

Osprey Publishing, part of Bloomsbury Publishing Plc
© 2016 Osprey Publishing Ltd

A CIP catalog record for this book is available from the British Library.

ISBN: 978 1 4728 1433 3
PDF e-book ISBN: 978 1 4728 1434 0
e-Pub ISBN: 978 1 4728 1435 7

Editorial by Ilios Publishing Ltd, Oxford, UK (www.iliospublishing.com)
Index by Alan Rutter
Typeset in Myriad Pro and Sabon
Maps by Bounford.com
3D bird's-eye views by The Black Spot
Battlescene illustrations by Peter Dennis
Originated by PDQ Media, Bungay, UK
Printed in China through World Print Ltd.

16 17 18 19 20   10 9 8 7 6 5 4 3 2 1

ARTIST'S NOTE

Readers may care to note that the original paintings from which the color
plates in this book were prepared are available for private sale. The
Publishers retain all reproduction copyright whatsoever. All enquiries
should be addressed to:

Peter Dennis, Fieldhead, The Park, Mansfield, Notts, NG18 2AT, UK
Email: magie.h@ntlworld.com

The Publishers regret that they can enter into no correspondence upon this
matter.

THE WOODLAND TRUST

Osprey Publishing are supporting the Woodland Trust, the UK's leading
woodland conservation charity, by funding the dedication of trees.

ACKNOWLEDGMENTS

Kathy Lloyd provided invaluable information on all matters equine. Dale
Benington provided pictures from his matchless collection of early site
photographs in Ohio and neighboring states, and John Stanton from his
collection of photographs of early fort sites across America. Carol Ely, Andy
Hite, Christine Kull, Stephanie Pouget-Papak, Patrick Schifferdecker, and
Christie Weininger generously contributed images from their museum
archives. Tom Fournier, Erin Worthy, and Robyn Zimmerman provided other
photographs. Mel Hankla, John MacLeod of Fort Malden Historic Site, Tim
Mclaughlin of the Erie Maritime Museum, and Michael Rupert generously
provided help in obtaining other photographs.

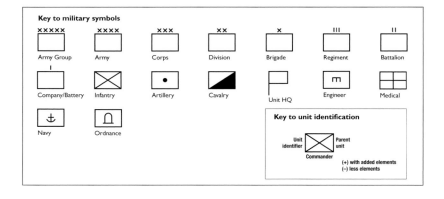

CONTENTS

The Northwest Frontier in 1812.

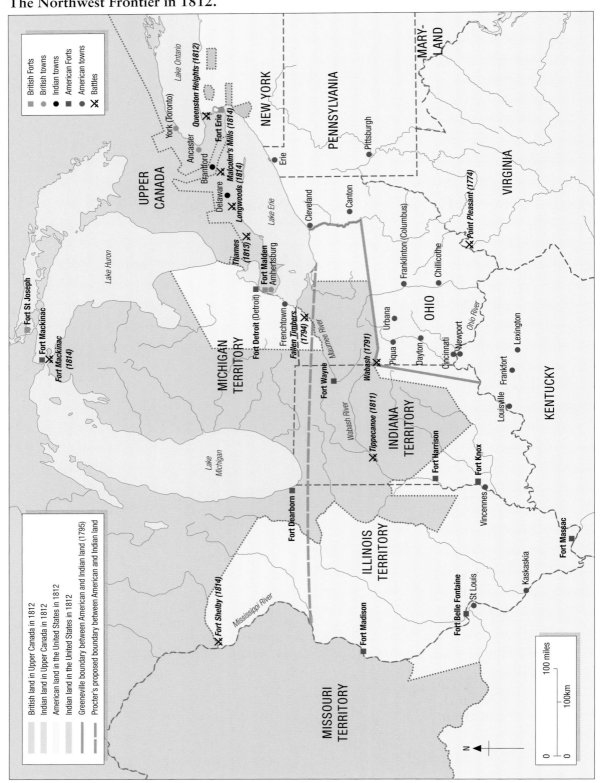

Legend:
- British Forts
- British towns
- Indian towns
- American Forts
- American towns
- Battles

British land in Upper Canada in 1812
Indian land in Upper Canada in 1812
American land in the United States in 1812
Indian land in the United States in 1812
Greeneville boundary between American and Indian land (1795)
Procter's proposed boundary between American and Indian land

MARY-LAND

NEW YORK

PENNSYLVANIA

VIRGINIA

UPPER CANADA

Lake Ontario

York (Toronto)
Queenston Heights (1812)
Ancaster
Fort Erie
Fort Erie (1814)
Brantford
Malcolm's Mills (1814)
Delaware
Longwoods (1814)
Erie
Pittsburgh
Point Pleasant (1774)

Lake Erie

Cleveland
Canton

Thames (1813)
Fort Malden
Amherstburg

Franklinton (Columbus)
Chillicothe

OHIO

Fort St Joseph

Lake Huron

Fort Mackinac
Fort Mackinac (1814)

Frenchtown
Fort Detroit (Detroit)
Failed Timbers (1794)
Maumee River

Urbana
Piqua
Dayton
Cincinnati
Newport

Ohio River

Lexington
Frankfort

MICHIGAN TERRITORY

Wabash (1791)

Fort Wayne

Wabash River

Tippecanoe (1811)

INDIANA TERRITORY

Louisville

KENTUCKY

Lake Michigan

Fort Harrison

Fort Knox

Fort Dearborn

Vincennes

Fort Massac

ILLINOIS TERRITORY

Kaskaskia

Fort Shelby (1814)

Mississippi River

Fort Madison

Fort Belle Fontaine
St Louis

MISSOURI TERRITORY

N

100 miles

100km

0

0

ORIGINS OF THE CAMPAIGN

The War of 1812 would be remembered in Britain as the American War, but it might as aptly have been called the Kentucky War. Although the state had only 5 percent of the American population, it provided 60 percent of the American soldiers in the war, and suffered 70 percent of the American casualties.

The Kentuckians fought on the American Northwest Frontier. Their goal was to end the continuing threat that the British in Canada would incite and support Indian attacks on American settlers in the area between the Ohio River and the Great Lakes. In the last of the Ohio Indian Wars, their effort culminated at the October 5, 1813 battle of the Thames River, which Canadians remember as the battle of Moraviantown. There Kentucky militiamen led by William Henry Harrison defeated a British and Indian army, and killed the famous Indian leader Tecumseh. After the peace treaty that followed, British support for the Indians ended, and raiding on the Northwest Frontier ceased.

STRATEGIC SITUATION

In 1812, the fourth year of the presidency of James Madison, about 8 million Americans lived in the nation's 18 states and five federal territories. On the Northwest Frontier, 400,000 lived in Kentucky and 250,000 in Ohio. Another 70,000 were in the Indiana, Illinois, and Michigan territories, and the Louisiana Territory, renamed in 1812 the Missouri Territory. The Northwest Frontier's largest urban centers were Lexington, in Kentucky, and Cincinnati, in Ohio, with populations of about 4,500 and 2,500 respectively.

Ruled by the Prince Regent, who in 1820 would become King George IV, Great Britain had a population of 19 million, of whom nearly 13 million lived in England. Another 400,000 lived in Lower and Upper Canada, where Lieutenant-General Sir George Prévost served as Governor General of the Canadas.

In Upper Canada, Brigadier-General Isaac Brock ruled as Prévost's Lieutenant Governor from York, a town of 700 that later would be called Toronto. After the Revolutionary War, 7,000 loyalist refugees had settled in the province. To expand the population, the government had in 1792 begun offering Americans generous grants of land in return for oaths of loyalty to the Crown. By 1812, about 90 percent of the 80,000 Upper Canada settlers were American immigrants or their descendants.

When the British left Detroit in 1796, the loyalist owners of this house had it moved across the Detroit River to Amherstburg. (Photo courtesy of Stephanie Pouget-Papak, Curator, Park House Museum)

Between the American Northwest Frontier and Upper Canada lay 300-mile long Lake Erie. Fed by Lake Huron, Lake St Clair, and the Detroit River, its waters flowed through the Niagara River, Lake Ontario, and the St Lawrence River to the Atlantic. The Detroit River separated the Michigan Territory, which had been occupied by Britain until 1796, from southwestern Upper Canada, which many called "Uppermost Canada."

About 13,000 settlers lived near the border. In the Michigan Territory, 5,000 American immigrants and descendants of French settlers lived between Frenchtown, which had about 50 structures, and Detroit, the territorial capital, which had more than 200. Across the river, nearly 8,000 Canadians lived in a crescent of settlement that curved clockwise from Lake Erie along the shores of the Detroit River and Lake St Clair and up the Thames River. The largest town was Amherstburg, which had 150 structures.

The Americans and Canadians near the Detroit River were far from any other centers of population. By rough, often impassable, roads, Detroit was more than 300 miles from Cincinnati, and Amherstburg as far from York. On Lake Erie, about 20 small vessels carried the mail and supplies from the nearest American port, Cleveland, which had 10 log structures, and from British Fort Erie.

The isolation of the Michigan and Uppermost Canada settlers encouraged amicable relations. Many had common relatives and business interests. But there

The remains of Fort Malden, also known as Fort Amherstburg, can be seen at Fort Malden National Historic Site in Amherstburg, Ontario. (Photograph by Dale Bennington)

were reminders that different nations claimed their allegiance. American Fort Detroit and British Fort Malden guarded the border. The guns of the British warship *Queen Charlotte* enforced peace on Lake Erie. Different laws governed life on opposite sides of the Detroit River. Slavery, for example, was banned in Ohio and the Indiana, Illinois, and Michigan territories, but legal in Upper Canada.

Many loyalist refugees in Uppermost Canada still frowned when they saw the American flag flying over Fort Detroit. In 1778, Alexander McKee, who had been the chief British agent for the Ohio Indians, had fled from Pittsburgh with the traders Matthew Elliott and Simon Girty. The three then had proved their value to the Crown by organizing and leading the Indians against the Americans for the next 16 years. McKee had died in 1799, but 73-year-old Elliott, who had succeeded McKee as head of the British Indian Department, lived south of Amherstburg on a large estate. The 71-year-old Girty, who had led the Indians in many raids and battles, had a house nearby.

More than 70,000 Indians lived in Ohio; the Indiana, Illinois, and Michigan territories; and Uppermost Canada. At Salem, in Ohio, and Moraviantown, in Uppermost Canada, the Christian Delaware prospered as farmers and artisans, manufacturers and traders. At their Ohio villages, many of Black Hoof's Shawnees and Tarhe's Wyandots also had begun living much like the settlers. It was the same with the Mohawks in Brantford, in Upper Canada, where John Norton had in 1807 succeeded the famous chief Joseph Brant as the tribe's leader.

But most of the Indians still followed the ways of their ancestors. The women, children, and slaves labored in fields around small tribal villages. The men devoted their time to hunting and war. From 1754 to 1762, Indian warriors had battled the American settlers in the French and Indian War, and from 1762 to 1764 in Pontiac's War. They had fought the Americans again at the October 10, 1774 battle of Point Pleasant, which had opened Kentucky to settlement, and from 1775 to 1783 during the Revolutionary War. Led by the great Miami war chief Little Turtle, they had destroyed the first US Army at the November 4, 1791 battle of the Wabash. But Anthony Wayne's new US Army had at last defeated them on August 20, 1794 at Fallen Timbers.

Wayne's August 7, 1795 Treaty of Greeneville had defined the boundary between American and Indian territory. But tribal leaders like Black Hoof, Tarhe, Little Turtle, and the Potawatomis Winamac and Five Medals had angered many Indians by selling the Americans land in later treaties. In 1809, two Shawnee brothers, the Prophet and Tecumseh, had commenced at Prophetstown in the Indiana Territory an attempt to create a union of all the Indian tribes east of the Mississippi River to oppose the Americans. The Potawatomi Main Poc also had begun leading warriors against American settlers in the Illinois Territory. On November 7, 1811, the Prophetstown Indians had attacked an American army led by the governor of the Indiana Territory, William Henry Harrison. The Indians' defeat at the battle of Tippecanoe had discredited the Prophet, but both Tecumseh and Main Poc remained eager for war with the Americans.

Elliott's rise to prominence began in 1774, when he was a trader living with the Shawnee. After Point Pleasant, the Shawnee commander Cornstalk dispatched him as a peace emissary to the invading Virginians. This coat belonged to Elliott. (Parks Canada Agency)

THE BEGINNING OF THE WAR

For 20 years, the United States had remained neutral as Britain had fought against Revolutionary, and then Napoleonic, France. But Britain had provoked the Americans by claiming, in a proclamation known as the "Orders in Council," a right to confiscate any American ship that traded with France. It had also infuriated them by forcibly seizing from American ships as Royal Navy deserters about 6,000 American sailors.

As war approached in early 1812, Secretary of War William Eustis asked William Hull, the governor of the Michigan Territory, to command the American army that would operate on the Detroit River border. To form the army, the Fort Detroit garrison and Michigan Territory militia would be reinforced by Lieutenant-Colonel James Miller's 4th US Infantry Regiment, which had fought at Tippecanoe; and three Ohio militia regiments, led by colonels Lewis Cass, James Findlay, and Duncan McArthur.

For service on the Northwest Frontier, Eustis also authorized the raising of five new regiments for the small American regular army. The famous Indian fighter Colonel Samuel Wells already had begun organizing the new 17th US Infantry Regiment. Colonel John Miller was to command the new 19th, Colonel Thomas Key Owings the 24th, Colonel George Paull the 27th, and Colonel William P. Anderson the 28th.

Few Indians, the Americans hoped, would fight with the British. Thousands were expected to confirm their neutrality at councils to be held at Brownstown, a Wyandot village in the Michigan Territory, and at the farm of the Indian agent John Johnston near Piqua in Ohio. But to protect the frontier, Eustis called upon Colonel William Russell. At 15, Russell had fought in his father's company at Point Pleasant. Twenty years later, he had led 275 Kentucky horsemen at Fallen Timbers. Now he was to command the US Army Rangers, 10 companies of experienced frontiersmen.

When Prévost learned of the growing threat of war, he urged the British Prime Minister Robert Jenkinson, 2nd Earl of Liverpool, to cancel the Orders in Council. Brock, however, prepared for battle. During the Revolutionary War, Britain had debated for two years whether to use Indians against the Americans. Brock, however, did not hesitate. Without them, he would have

Dickson's trading post was 9 miles northwest of present Baudette, Minnesota. The photograph shows a reconstructed North West Company trading post near Pine City, Minnesota. (Courtesy of the Minnesota Historical Society's North West Company Fur Post, Pine City)

available to defend his province only a few hundred British regulars, and Upper Canada militiamen who were as likely to fight with the Americans as against them.

To recruit Indian allies, Brock turned to Elliott and the prominent trader Robert Dickson. Since 1808, when Elliott had been asked to return from retirement to head the British Indian Department, he had maintained relationships with chiefs like John Norton, Tecumseh, and Main Poc that would produce many warriors. Dickson, whose North West Company had trading posts as far west as what is now British Columbia, could recruit still more. Altogether, Elliott estimated, Brock might have as many as 4,400 warriors.

On May 25, Hull assumed command of Cass's, Findlay's, and McArthur's regiments in Dayton. After James Miller's regiment arrived, his army went forward. Its first task was to cut a supply road to Detroit from Urbana, the forwardmost of the populous Ohio settlements. Along the course of Hull's Road, it built forts McArthur and Findlay, at modern Kenton and Findlay, Ohio.

On June 18, the United States declared war. When the news reached Amherstburg on June 28, Tecumseh, Main Poc, and the famous Wyandot chief Roundhead were there. They immediately agreed to fight with the British.

On July 5, Hull's army reached Detroit. Two days later, he attended the Brownstown council, where Winamac, Five Medals, and many other chiefs promised to remain neutral in the conflict. On July 12, he led his army across the Detroit River.

In Uppermost Canada, Hull issued a proclamation announcing that the Canadians' institutions and laws would be respected while the Americans remained. Many Canadians hoped that the American occupation would be permanent. Between July 13 and 16, McArthur led 175 dragoons to Chatham. Settlers as far as Delaware, he reported, were planning to form militia companies to fight with the Americans.

All that remained was to capture Fort Malden. After small skirmishes with British and Indian forces, Hull concluded on July 21 that he would need to reduce the British fortress using two 24lb guns mounted at Fort Detroit. To transport the pieces, which each weighed more than 2 tons, special carriages and barges would have to be constructed.

This gun overlooking Lake Huron is at Fort Mackinac, now a museum in Mackinac, Michigan. (Photograph by John Stanton)

The British had little hope that Malden could be held. Only 200 regulars from the 41st Regiment of Foot, 10th Royal Veteran Battalion, and Royal Regiment of Artillery were available to defend it. Indians were arriving daily, but there still were few. The Canadian militiamen could not be relied upon. Loyal Captain Daniel Springer reported to Brock on July 23: "I dare not trust them on any occasion whatever, and conceive myself in danger." "My situation," a worried Brock wrote on July 29, "is most

critical, not from anything the enemy can do, but from the disposition of the people. The population, believe me, is essentially bad."

But the British commander's despair was premature. The day before Brock recorded his view of the Canadians he governed, Hull received devastating news from northern Michigan. From British Fort Joseph, a force of 200 soldiers and 400 of Dickson's Indians had attacked American Fort Mackinac on July 17. Its 60 American defenders, unaware that war had been declared, had yielded the formidable fortress without resistance. Hull immediately asked Winamac to take to Captain Nathan Heald, the commandant at Fort Dearborn, an order to withdraw his garrison to Fort Wayne.

An emboldened Colonel Henry Procter, whom Brock had sent to organize the defense of Fort Malden, gambled that Hull now would not attack his stronghold. He sent most of his regulars, and warriors under Tecumseh and Main Poc, across the Detroit River to cut Hull's line of communication and supply. On August 5, they attacked a force of 150 Ohio militiamen near Brownstown, killing 17 and wounding 12. The bodies of the dead, Hull's scouts reported, now were impaled on posts on the road to Ohio.

On August 7, the American artillery was ready for the assault on Malden. At a council of his officers, Hull ordered the attack to go forward. But a few hours later, his bewildered lieutenants received a new order. The Americans, he announced, would retreat from Uppermost Canada.

The news panicked the pro-American Canadians. "It was a heart-rending sight," said an American in Detroit, "to see these poor fellows flocking down to the river and begging General Hull to remain and protect them or take them with him. When they could not get in the boats, numbers of them jumped into the river and swam over."

That evening, Winamac arrived at Fort Dearborn. Heald, he advised, should ignore Hull's order. The Americans would be massacred if they left the fort. But Heald was unwilling to disobey his commander's instructions. The garrison, he announced, would immediately begin destroying Fort Dearborn's supplies and munitions, and leave the fort on August 15.

On August 8, Hull learned that thousands of American regulars and militiamen soon would be coming to reinforce his army. That day, he sent James Miller, 280 regulars, 300 Ohio militiamen, and two guns to keep open the road from Ohio. On August 9, 200 British regulars and militiamen led by Captain Adam Muir, and 300 Indians led by Tecumseh and Main Poc, attacked Miller's force at Monguagon. In the American victory that followed, Muir and Tecumseh were wounded, and 40 Indians were killed, many by British fire.

As the British and Indians were fleeing from Monguagon, William Wells, the

At the July 20, 1814 Bloody Assize of Ancaster, eight Upper Canada settlers were executed for aiding the Americans. This broadsheet, issued by the government of Upper Canada, lists 380 Canadian men who escaped to the United States. (Archives of Ontario, RG 22-3782, Treason Poster)

American Indian agent at Fort Wayne, learned of Hull's order to abandon Fort Dearborn. Wells, an adopted Miami, had been an Indian commander at Wabash. Then, after meeting his brother, Colonel Samuel Wells, he had returned to Kentucky and served as Wayne's chief scout.

The summer of 1812 had brought Wells only bad news. On July 14, his father-in-law, Little Turtle, had died. Then had come word of the fall of Mackinac. If the Americans tried to march from Fort Dearborn to Fort Wayne, he believed, they would be massacred – and Samuel Wells's daughter Rebecca, Heald's wife, would be among them. With 30 Miami warriors, Wells raced to Heald's fort.

The American victory at Monguagon did not raise Hull's spirits. On August 12, he ordered Miller to return to Detroit. That day, Cass later wrote to Eustis, he, Findlay, and McArthur "were informed through a medium which admitted of no doubt, that the general had stated that a capitulation would be necessary." The three shocked Ohio colonels secured the agreement of 80 senior officers and prominent Detroit residents that Hull must be replaced.

Cass then drafted a secret letter from the three colonels to Ohio Governor Return J. Meigs, the nearest person with authority to remove the American commander. Meigs, they pled, must march to Detroit immediately with 2,000 men. In a desperate postscript, Cass added: "Believe all the bearer will tell you. Believe it, however it may astonish you, as much as if told by one of us. Even a c----------- is talked of by the c-------- -------. The bearer will supply the vacancy. On you we depend." The words left for the messenger to reveal were "capitulation" and "commanding general."

By then, Prévost had received the news he had hoped for. Liverpool had cancelled the Orders in Council. Confident that the action would cause the Americans to end the war before serious hostilities commenced, he had contacted Henry Dearborn, the commanding general of the US Army, who was in Albany, New York. Dearborn had agreed to a ceasefire from August 20 through September 10 while the American government considered the news.

Desperate to avoid the fall of Malden before August 20, Brock had hurried west with reinforcements. When he arrived on August 13, he learned that the situation had changed completely. The Americans had left Canada, the pro-American Canadians were fleeing, and Indians were arriving in large numbers.

On August 14, Brock reviewed his 330 British regulars and 400 Canadian militiamen. But all eyes were on another sight: the 600 terrifying, painted Indian warriors who had joined them. They looked, recalled the frightened Amherstburg resident Thomas Verchères de Boucherville, like they were "standing at the gates of Hell, with the gates thrown open to let the damned out for an hour's recreation on earth."

Cass later would serve as governor of the Michigan Territory, US senator from Michigan, US ambassador to France, US secretary of war, and US secretary of state, and be defeated in the 1848 election for US president by Zachary Taylor. This Daniel Chester French statue of Cass is in the US Capitol. (Architect of the Capitol)

The British commander, however, recaptured his audience's attention with an announcement that stunned his officers. His force was outnumbered by the 2,100 Americans across the river. It was outgunned by their 33 artillery pieces. It lacked even scaling ladders to ascend Fort Detroit's 22ft-high walls, which rose above a moat 8ft deep. But it nonetheless would attack.

When the British began occupying battle positions across the Detroit River from the American fortress, the Ohio colonels realized that they could not wait for Meigs to arrive. They "determined as a last resort," Cass told Eustis, "to incur the responsibility of divesting the general from his command."

On August 15, Hull, who knew nothing about Prévost's and Dearborn's imminent ceasefire, received a message from Brock. "It is far from my intention to join in a war of extermination," the British commander wrote as if he could read Hull's mind, "but you must be aware that the numerous body of Indians who have attached themselves to my troops will be beyond my control the moment the contest commences."

THE AMERICAN DISASTER

On August 16, Johnston's Indian council began at his farm. Black Hoof, Tarhe, and other chiefs announced that their Indians would remain neutral in the war. But news of the capture of Fort Mackinac and of Hull's withdrawal from Canada had spread quickly. Although 3,000 Indians had been expected, only 750 had appeared.

Bad news from Fort Wayne then arrived at Johnston's farm. Wells had reached Fort Dearborn the night before the planned departure, just after Heald had destroyed the last of the fort's ammunition. On August 15, 66 American soldiers, 9 women and 18 children had left the fort. They had found waiting a mile and a half ahead the Potawatomi Mad Sturgeon and 500 warriors. The Americans had killed 15 of the Potawatomis and wounded Mad Sturgeon, but the Indians had killed 38 of the soldiers, 2 of the women,

John Johnston's farm is now a museum near Piqua, Ohio. (Courtesy of the Johnston Farm and Indian Agency)

and 12 of the children, and taken the rest as captives.

Rebecca Heald, who had survived with seven wounds, had seen her uncle fall. He had removed his coat and shirt, she remembered, and painted himself black with moistened gunpowder. Then Wells had died as a Miami, screaming insults at the Potawatomis he fought.

Catastrophic news from Detroit then followed. Before the Ohio colonels could remove him, Hull had on August 16 surrendered Fort Detroit without firing a shot. "I have done what my conscience directed," Hull had said. "I have saved Detroit and the territory from the horrors of an Indian massacre."

Hull, Brock announced when he entered Detroit, had not just surrendered his fortress and army. He had ceded to Great Britain the territory he governed. "The Territory of Michigan was this day by capitulation ceded to the arms of His Britannic Majesty without any other condition than the protection of private property," Brock proclaimed. "The laws heretofore in existence shall continue in force until His Majesty's pleasure be known."

Brock's soldiers and warriors were ecstatic. It was British practice to sell property seized in a captured town, and to distribute the proceeds among the occupying army's officers and soldiers. From Detroit, every British soldier was to get a share as large as six months' salary. The Indians, the British commander wrote, "appear determined to continue the contest until they obtain the Ohio for a boundary."

A horrified Prévost, who feared the effect of Brock's action on his attempt to end the war, urged the British commander to withdraw his force from the Michigan Territory immediately. He would not, Brock responded. "Such a measure," he wrote, "would most probably be followed by a total extinction of the population on that side of the river."

Brock then took advantage of the triumph for which he would receive a knighthood and promotion to major-general. On August 29, he wrote directly to the Earl of Liverpool, urging the British government to adopt an aggressive policy on the Northwest Frontier. There should be no peace, Brock said, without the establishment of an area to be occupied only by Indians, and ruled by leaders allied with Britain. At a minimum, he said, the Americans must surrender to the Indians all lands beyond the Greeneville Treaty line.

Prévost's worst fears were soon realized. Enraged by their humiliation, the Americans ignored Liverpool's cancellation of the Orders in Council. On the day Brock wrote to the Prime Minister, President Madison ordered the US Navy to build a fleet to take control of Lake Erie.

The British commander then returned to York, leaving Procter in command. The Indians, Procter learned, now were gathering to attack Fort

TOP
For his action, Hull would be courtmartialed and given a death sentence, which Madison commuted. In this message, Hull informed Brock that he would surrender. (Archives of Ontario, F775, Hull to Brock, First Message)

BOTTOM
This list shows the distribution of prize shares from the capture of Detroit to the 19 men in Captain Jean Barthe's Canadian militia company. (Archives of Ontario, F895, Box MU, Prize List)

Wayne. As soon as the ceasefire ended, he concluded, he would dispatch a British force with artillery to reduce the stronghold.

For the most exposed American settlers, there was terror; and for the rest on the Northwest Frontier, gloom. But there were glimmers of hope. The American disaster had not shaken the resolve of Black Hoof and Tarhe to keep their Shawnees and Wyandots neutral. Colonel George Adams, who had been the chief American scout at Wabash, had collected 700 men in the Dayton area to relieve Fort Wayne. Findlay, after being released from captivity, had assembled 350 more in Cincinnati.

Much of the force that was to reinforce Hull, moreover, had been mustered. Ohio Brigadier-General Anselm Tupper and 1,200 militiamen were camped 20 miles southeast of Chillicothe. Samuel Wells and 250 men of the new 17th US Infantry Regiment were in Cincinnati.

Powerful Kentucky militia forces also were on the way. Brigadier-General John Payne was approaching Cincinnati with Lieutenant-Colonel John Allen's 600-man regiment; Lieutenant-Colonel John Scott's 475 men; and the 675-man regiment of Lieutenant-Colonel William Lewis, who had led a company at Fallen Timbers. With them were Colonel Richard M. Johnson's 450 mounted riflemen and Captain William Garrard's 80 dragoons. Coming behind them were Lieutenant-Colonel Joshua Barbee's 500-man regiment, Lieutenant-Colonel William Jennings's 600 men, Lieutenant-Colonel John Pogue's 575 men, and Lieutenant-Colonel James Simrall's 280 dragoons.

The popular and politically powerful James Wilkinson, who had been Wayne's second-in-command at Fallen Timbers, had demanded leadership of the Kentucky militia who would fight in the war. But Governor Charles Scott had led 1,500 Kentuckians at Fallen Timbers, and governor-elect Isaac Shelby, who had been in 1794 the state's first governor, had sent Scott and his men. Wilkinson, they knew, was a villain, who had tried to sabotage the Fallen Timbers campaign. They offered the command to Harrison, who accepted.

After leaving the adopted Delaware John Gibson to serve as governor of the Indiana Territory in his absence, Harrison met with Brigadier-General James Winchester, the senior US Army officer on the Northwest Frontier. Winchester, Harrison suggested, should continue organizing the new 19th, 24th, 27th and 28th regiments while he led the available forces forward to Fort Wayne. Winchester agreed.

On August 29, as Brock was writing to the Earl of Liverpool, and Madison ordering construction of a Lake Erie fleet, Harrison addressed the Kentuckians who had arrived in Cincinnati. They would march at once to Fort Wayne, he announced. "It appeared to me, Sir," Harrison wrote to Secretary of War Eustis, "necessary that someone should undertake the general direction of affairs here and I have done it."

Six weeks after leaving Detroit, Brock fell at the October 13, 1812 battle of Queenston Heights. This 1883 George Theodore Berthon portrait depicts the bold British commander. (Government of Ontario Art Collection, 694158. Courtesy of Archives of Ontario)

The Detroit River area of operations.

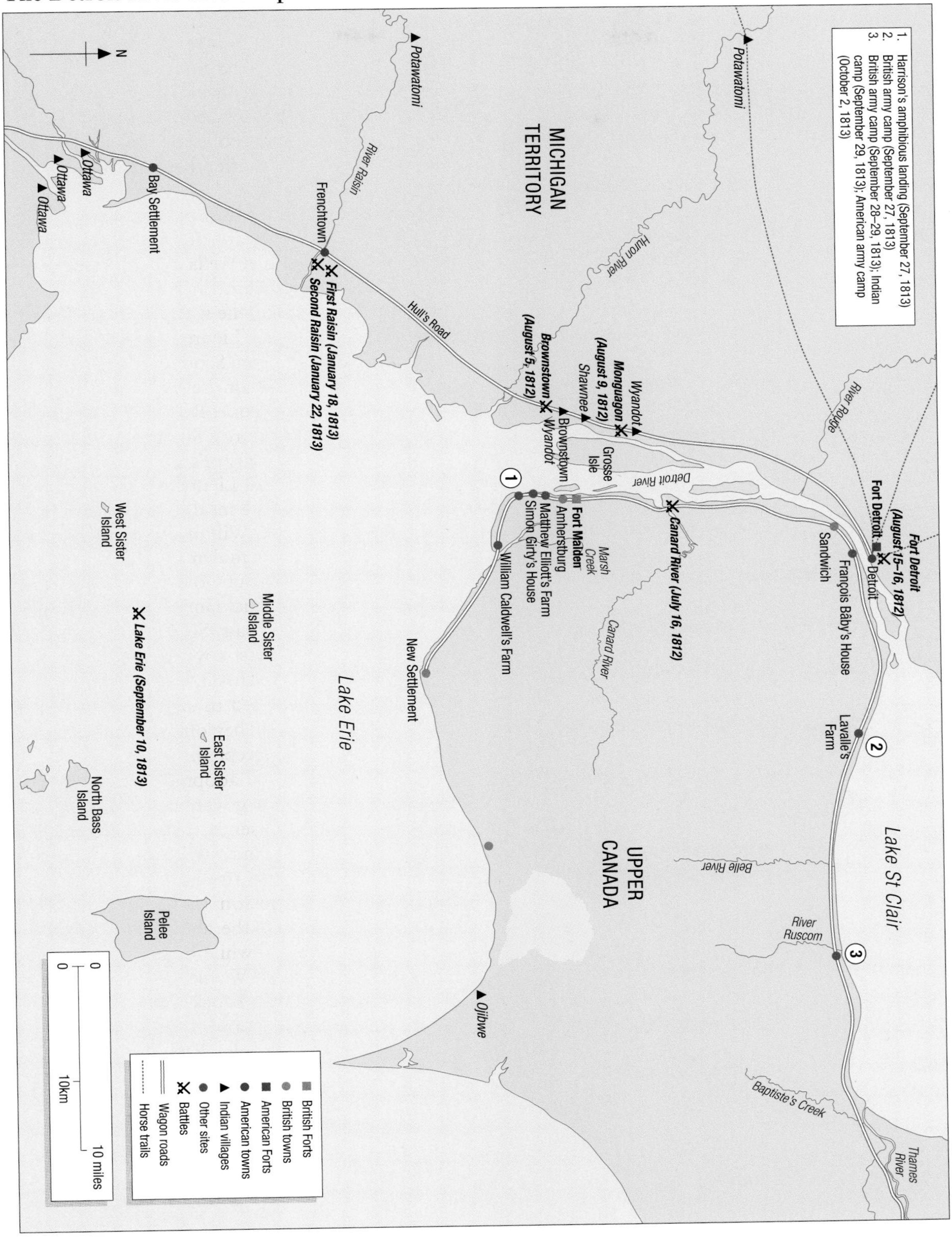

Legend:
- British Forts
- British towns
- American towns
- American Forts
- Indian villages
- Other sites
- Battles
- Wagon roads
- Horse trails

1. Harrison's amphibious landing (September 27, 1813)
2. British army camp (September 27, 1813)
3. British army camp (September 28–29, 1813); Indian camp (September 29, 1813); American army camp (October 2, 1813)

MICHIGAN TERRITORY

UPPER CANADA

Lake Erie

Lake St Clair

Detroit River

River Raisin

Huron River

River Rouge

Canard River

Belle River

Thames River

Baptiste's Creek

Potawatomi
Potawatomi
Ottawa
Ottawa
Ottawa
Bay Settlement

Frenchtown
First Raisin (January 18, 1813)
Second Raisin (January 22, 1813)

Hull's Road

Brownstown (August 5, 1812)
Monguagon (August 9, 1812)
Shawnee
Wyandot
Brownstown
Wyandot
Grosse Isle

Fort Detroit
(August 15–16, 1812)
Fort Detroit
Detroit
Sandwich
François Bâby's House

Canard River (July 16, 1812)
Marsh Creek
Amherstburg
Fort Malden
Matthew Elliott's Farm
Simon Girty's House
William Caldwell's Farm

New Settlement

West Sister Island
Middle Sister Island
East Sister Island
North Bass Island

Lake Erie (September 10, 1813)

Pelee Island

Lavalle's Farm

River Ruscom

Ojibwe

0   10Km
0   10 miles

15

CHRONOLOGY

1812

May 25	Hull assumes command of the American Army of the Northwest.
June 18	The US declares war on Britain.
July 12	Hull's army invades Upper Canada.
July 17	The British capture Fort Mackinac.
August 5	The battle of Brownstown.
August 9	The battle of Monguagon.
August 12	The Americans leave Upper Canada.
August 15	The Fort Dearborn Massacre.
August 16	Hull surrenders Detroit.
August 20–September 10	Prévost's ceasefire.
September 4–5	Attack on Fort Harrison.
September 5–8	Attack on Fort Madison.
September 5–11	Attack on Fort Wayne.
September 14–October 3	Muir's expedition to Fort Wayne.
September 24	Harrison receives command of the Army of the Northwest.
September 29	The battle of Marblehead Peninsula.
November 14	The battle of Hull's Crossing.
November 22	The battle of Wildcat Creek.
December 18	The battle of Mississinewa.

1813

January 18	The first battle of the Raisin.
January 22	The second battle of the Raisin.
April 28–May 9	The first siege of Fort Meigs.
June 21	Franklinton council with the Ohio Indians.
July 21–28	The second siege of Fort Meigs.
August 1–2	Attack on Fort Stephenson.
September 10	The battle of Lake Erie.
September 27	Harrison's army lands in Canada.
September 30	Richard M. Johnson's regiment reaches Detroit.
October 2	Harrison begins the pursuit of Procter.
October 5	The battle of the Thames.

1814

March 14	The battle of Longwoods.
November 6	The battle of Malcolm's Mills.

1815

February 18	The war ends with US Senate approval of the Treaty of Ghent.

OPPOSING COMMANDERS

AMERICAN AND ALLIED INDIAN COMMANDERS

Major-General William Henry Harrison, 40 in 1813, led the American army that fought at Thames. A son of a signer of the Declaration of Independence, avid reader of Greek and Latin literature, gifted violinist, and author of one of the first works on American archaeology, he also was a Northwest Frontier settler, who inspired the enthusiastic loyalty of the often rough Kentucky frontiersmen he led. A bold and imaginative commander, he had learned as an aide to Anthony Wayne during the Fallen Timbers campaign how to conduct operations against the Indians. He would in 1840 be elected the 9th President of the United States, but die soon after his inauguration.

Harrison's staff included **Brigadier-General Lewis Cass**, who had served under Hull as an Ohio militia colonel, and **US Navy Master Commandant Oliver Hazard Perry**. After his great victory at the September 10, 1813 battle of Lake Erie, Perry had asked to accompany Harrison as his aide-de-camp.

Harrison's principal subordinate was 63-year-old **Isaac Shelby**, the Governor of Kentucky, who served as his second-in-command. Shelby, who had led a company at Point Pleasant, had won fame as a commander at the October 7, 1780 battle of King's Mountain. Shelby's staff included his aides **John Adair** and **John J. Crittenden**. Adair, who had led the Kentuckians at the November 6, 1792 battle of Fort St Clair, would lead 1,000 men from the state at the January 8, 1815 battle of New Orleans, and later be elected governor of Kentucky. Crittenden, another Kentucky governor, would twice serve as US Attorney General, and, as a US Senator in 1860, would be a leading figure in efforts to avoid the Civil War.

Harrison, judged Colonel Richard M. Johnson, had "the confidence of the forces without parallel in our history, except in the case of Gen. Washington in the Revolution." This 1850 photograph of a daguerreotype shows Harrison shortly before his death in 1841. (Author's collection)

Shelby's senior subordinates commanded his two divisions. **Major-General Joseph Desha**, who led one, would, after first losing to Adair, also be a Kentucky governor. Desha's principal subordinates, who led his two brigades, were **Colonel James Allen** and **Brigadier-General Samuel Caldwell**. **Major-General William Henry** commanded Shelby's other division. His principal subordinates, who led his three brigades, were **Colonel George Trotter**, who had fought as a captain at the December 18, 1812, battle of Mississinewa; **Brigadier-General George King**, and **Brigadier-General David Chiles**.

Colonel Richard M. Johnson, aged 33, led an oversized regiment of Kentucky volunteers that alone fought most of the battle. In 1836, he would become the 9th Vice-President of the United States. He personally led his regiment's 2d Battalion against the Indians as his second-in-command, his brother **Lieutenant-Colonel James Johnson**, led the 1st Battalion against the British.

Colonel George Paull, commander of the 27th US Infantry Regiment, led two US Army infantry companies at the battle. **Major Eleazar Wood** of the US Army Corps of Engineers commanded the artillery.

John and William Conner, Delaware traders in the Indiana Territory, led the warriors from their tribe in Harrison's army. The famous chief **Black Hoof**, who had commanded the Indians at the August 8, 1780 battle of Peckuwe, led the Shawnees. The celebrated chief **Tarhe**, who had been wounded at Fallen Timbers, commanded the Wyandots.

BRITISH AND ALLIED INDIAN COMMANDERS

Aged 50 in 1813, **Major-General Henry Procter** had served as a lieutenant during the Revolutionary War, and by 1812 risen to the rank of lieutenant-colonel in the 41st Regiment of Foot. He then succeeded Brigadier-General Isaac Brock as commander of British forces in Uppermost Canada. After his victory at the January 22, 1813 second battle of the Raisin, he was promoted to brigadier, and then major-general.

Procter's staff included **Captain Matthew Dixon** of the Corps of Royal Engineers, and **Lieutenant-Colonel François Bâby**, the commander of the Amherstburg area Upper Canada militia. Dixon, who supervised the army's construction of fortifications, was wounded at the August 1–2, 1813 battle of Fort Stephenson.

Procter's senior British Army commander was **Lieutenant-Colonel Augustus Warburton**, a veteran of campaigns in Surinam and Portugal, who led the 41st Regiment of Foot. Warburton's principal subordinates were **Captain Adam Muir**, who commanded the regiment's 1st Battalion, and **Lieutenant-Colonel William Evans**, who led the 2nd Battalion. Muir, a "ranker-officer," had risen to his command after enlistment as a private rather than by purchase of a commission. He was wounded at the August 9, 1812 battle of Monguagon, and again at Fort Stephenson. **Lieutenant Felix Troughton** of the Royal Artillery Regiment, who was wounded at the second battle of the Raisin, led the British artillery units. **Ensign John Richardson** of the light company of the 41st, aged 17 in 1813, later would become the first internationally renowned Canadian novelist.

Procter's Canadian subordinates included the commanders of two Upper Canada militia units. **Captain Thomas Coleman** led the army's horsemen, the

This 1973 C. H. J. Forster portrait depicts Procter. (Parks Canada Agency)

Canadian Light Dragoons. **Colonel William Caldwell** commanded Caldwell's Rangers, a light infantry unit that fought with the army's Indian allies. Caldwell had led similar units in fighting in Ohio during the Revolutionary War, and at Fallen Timbers.

Canadian **Lieutenant-Colonel Matthew Elliott,** the Superintendent of the British Indian Department, served at the battle as Procter's principal liaison with the army's Indian allies. His chief subordinates were two sons of Colonel William Caldwell: **Captain William Caldwell** and **Captain Billy Caldwell.** Billy Caldwell (Sauganash), who had a Potawatomi mother, was wounded at the battle. After succeeding Elliott as Superintendent of the Indian Department, he would in 1818 emigrate to the United States and lead a band of 2,000 Potawatomis.

The celebrated Shawnee **Tecumseh** generally commanded the allied Indians at Thames. The 45-year-old commander, who fell at the battle, personally led the left wing of the Indian formation. His immediate subordinates included the Potawatomi chiefs **Mad Sturgeon** (Nuscotomeg) and **Shabbona**, and **Splitlog**, brother of the famous, recently deceased, Wyandot commander Roundhead. Mad Sturgeon had led the Indians at the August 15, 1812 Fort Dearborn Massacre. In the Indian center, **Naiwash** led the Ottawas, and **Winepagon**, who fell at the battle, the Ojibwes. In the Indian right wing, **Oshawana**, also known as John Naudee, and Peckickee, a signer of the Greeneville Treaty who died at the battle, commanded the Ojibwes. **Four Legs** (Ochekka) and **Naw Kaw** led the Winnebagos.

OPPOSING FORCES

THE AMERICAN ARMY

Harrison's 3,000-man American army at Thames contained units of five types. The first three were his regular infantry, 120 men in two companies from the 24th and 27th US Infantry regiments; his artillery, 10 men from the 2d US Artillery Regiment with two 6lb guns; and his allied Indians, comprising 150 Ohio Delawares, Shawnees, and Wyandots.

Harrison's other 2,720 men were Kentucky mounted militiamen. Colonel Richard Johnson's Regiment of Kentucky Mounted Infantry Volunteers, 960 horsemen who had enlisted for six months, provided about 90 percent of the Americans actually in combat. The other 1,760 mounted militiamen, who had enlisted for two months' service, were in five two-regiment brigades led by Kentucky Governor Isaac Shelby. Shelby's men, who had left their horses in Ohio, fought on foot. Dressed at the battle in the black hats and hunting frocks of frontiersmen, Johnson's men were distinguishable from Shelby's because they had in their hats white plumes with tips died red, and wore black hunting frocks with red fringe rather than blue with red fringe.

By the time of the battle, many Americans doubted that militiamen ever could serve as adequate substitutes for US Army soldiers. Harrison, however, had seen the Kentuckians fight at Fallen Timbers and Tippecanoe. They were, he judged, "superior to any militia that took the field in modern times." The Indians shared his view. A warrior at Frenchtown, a resident recalled, was unconcerned at the approach of American militiamen until they came into view. "Kentuck. By God," he shouted, and retreated to the woods.

The Model 1803 Harper's Ferry Flintlock Rifle was the first mass-produced American rifled firearm. The weapon was 48in. long, weighed 9lb, and fired 54-caliber balls. (Courtesy of the National Firearms Museum/ National Rifle Association)

American operations against the Indians.

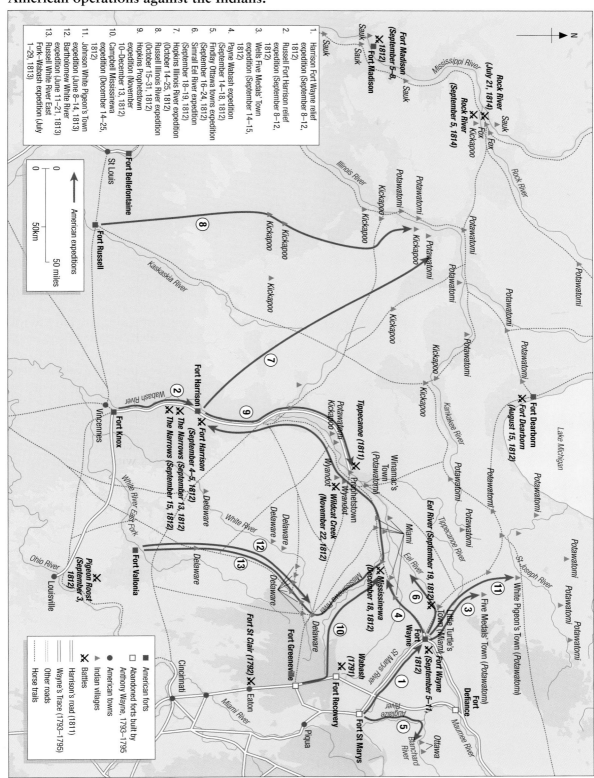

1. Harrison Fort Wayne relief expedition (September 8–12, 1812).
2. Russell Wabash expedition (September 8–12, 1812).
3. Wells Five Medals' Town expedition (September 14–15, 1812).
4. Payne Wabash expedition (September 14–18, 1812).
5. Findlay Ottawa towns expedition (September 16–24, 1812).
6. Simrall Eel River expedition (September 18–19, 1812).
7. Hopkins Illinois River expedition (October 14–25, 1812).
8. Russell Illinois River expedition (October 15–31, 1812).
9. Hopkins Prophetstown expedition (November 10–December 13, 1812).
10. Campbell Mississinewa expedition (December 14–25, 1812).
11. Johnson White Pigeon's Town expedition (June 8–14, 1813).
12. Bartholomew White River expedition (June 11–21, 1813).
13. Russell White River East Fork–Wabash expedition (July 1–29, 1813).

N

0   50km
0   50 miles

American expeditions

- ■ American forts
- □ Abandoned forts built by Anthony Wayne, 1793–1795
- ● American towns
- ▶ Indian villages
- ✕ Battles
- ——— Harrison's road (1811)
- ——— Wayne's Trace (1793–1795)
- ——— Other roads
- ········ Horse trails

Most of the Kentuckians carried their own firearms, 52-caliber long rifles that fired lead balls. Minimally competent riflemen could hit a target the size of a man's head at 100 yards. Others, however, chose weapons available to them after enlistment. Some chose a different rifle, the Model 1803 Harper's Ferry Flintlock Rifle. The weapon, although less accurate than their usual rifles, was about a foot shorter, and 2lb lighter. A few chose Springfield Model 1795 smoothbore muskets, which, when fitted with bayonets, could be used as short lances. For close combat, many of the Kentucky officers carried sabers and pistols. Soldiers carried as edged weapons tomahawks and butchers' knives.

The Kentuckians' formations and tactics had grown from experience in fighting Indians in the western woods. At Point Pleasant, they had learned that even the best riflemen were overmatched on foot when they faced an equal number of warriors. "To stand and fight them in regular order," wrote Captain Robert McAfee, who led one of Johnson's companies, "only exposes the man and hazards the victory. For in such a case, they will kill two to one of the best marksmen that can be opposed to them."

But during the Revolutionary War, the Kentuckians had discovered the advantages of a new tactic in Indian warfare: fighting on horseback. They then had learned how to exploit their mobility while mounted to surround bodies of Indian warriors, who upon their approach fled and scattered. "The best method," wrote McAfee, "is to outflank them, rush upon them, drive them from their lurking places, and pursue them closely."

Commanded by officers they had elected, the performance of the mounted riflemen depended to a very high degree on the quality of their leaders. These fiercely independent woodsmen were capable of producing stunning victories. But their eagerness to prove their bravery also could generate spectacular defeats. "It rarely occurs," Harrison said in a general order rebuking them, "that a general has to complain of the excessive ardor of his men, yet such appears always to be the case whenever the Kentucky militia are engaged."

The Kentuckians, British Ensign John Richardson observed, brought to a battlefield "an air of savageness." They also had adopted the Indian practice of taking the scalps of enemy warriors they killed. Stung by American complaints about the actions of Britain's Indian allies, British propagandists sometimes claimed that the Kentuckians were cruel savages. They enjoyed, asserted the imaginative Reverend John Strachan, who would become the first Anglican Bishop of Toronto, "burning warriors alive as a pastime." The propaganda sometimes created expectations that the Kentuckians could not fulfill. While being paraded with other Kentucky prisoners in Quebec, an amused Private William Atherton heard a woman remark to her companion, "Why they look just like other people."

An excellent corps of scouts guided the Americans in operations. The most notable were the Shawnees Anthony Shane and Johnny Logan, and the Michigan Territory settlers James Knaggs and Peter Navarre. At 77 years of age, Navarre retrieved his War of 1812 dress and weapons to recreate his appearance as one of Harrison's scouts in this 1867 photograph. (Courtesy of the Monroe County Historical Museum)

THE BRITISH AND INDIAN ARMY

Almost all of Procter's 1,350 men were in either the British 41st Regiment of Foot or Indian units. The British regulars wore 7in.-high, black "stovepipe" shakos with brass plates and worsted plumes, and leather "neck stocks" designed to keep their heads raised. They had red wool coatees with crossed white belts, with either white summer or blue-gray winter trousers and gaiters. They carried 75-caliber Indian pattern "Brown Bess" smoothbore, flintlock muskets, which could be fitted with 18in.-long bayonets.

British regiments had two 10-company battalions. They formed in battalion lines, usually in two ranks, in either "close order," standing shoulder to shoulder, or in "open order," about a yard apart. In battle, they were to fire mass volleys of their muskets, at a rate of three to four volleys per minute, or charge with bayonets. On their flanks were the battalion's elite companies, the "light company" on the left, and the grenadier company on the right. At Thames, Procter had 475 men of the 41st, including one light and one grenadier company.

British regulars had proven in countless engagements their steadiness in combat. But harshly disciplined, and stationed near the American border, the men of the 41st often were tempted to desert. Some were deaf to reports that boundless opportunity awaited them in America. Private Shadrack Byfield of the light company, a weaver by trade, rejected an American friend's suggestion that he leave the regiment's ranks. She said, Byfield remembered, "that if I deserted and went into the States, I should do well. I told her I could not desert my colours; and, that I hoped to see old England again."

But many others succumbed. In 1804, Brock pursued seven across the border into New York, and captured and executed them. In 1807, an armed mob thwarted Captain Adam Muir's attempt to seize a deserter in Detroit.

These Canadian 41st Regiment re-enactors, who invaded Ohio for the bicentennial celebration of the siege of Fort Meigs, are in Maumee, where this marker commemorates their unit. (Courtesy of the 41st Regiment of Foot Living History Group)

Trained since boyhood to endure discomfort and pain, Procter's 800 Indian warriors were masters of the skills needed for combat in the woods. They carried firearms of many types, mostly smoothbore muskets, and also used bows and arrows, tomahawks, and war clubs.

Led by superb commanders, they fought in small units using tactics so familiar that warriors usually could act effectively without receiving specific orders. They always attempted to surround enemy forces, no matter how greatly they were outnumbered. They then tried to compress the encirclement, and to surround separately any enemy units that escaped.

At Thames, the Indian force contained warriors from many western tribes, who spoke different languages and had very different customs. Some were familiar with the settlers. Others were from areas where English was seldom, if ever, heard. The diversity of their warriors hindered the ability of the Indian commanders to apply their usual tactics.

Terrifying when dressed for battle, the Indians sought to intimidate their enemies by cruel conduct. By the time of Thames, many had rejected practices such as torturing wounded prisoners, and killing enemy women and children.

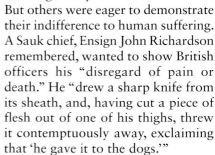

But others were eager to demonstrate their indifference to human suffering. A Sauk chief, Ensign John Richardson remembered, wanted to show British officers his "disregard of pain or death." He "drew a sharp knife from its sheath, and, having cut a piece of flesh out of one of his thighs, threw it contemptuously away, exclaiming that 'he gave it to the dogs.'"

Richardson was a defender of Brock's decision to use Indian warriors against the Americans. "The law of self-preservation," he wrote, "was our guide, and scrupulous, indeed, must be the power that would have hesitated at such a moment in its choice." But even Richardson's scruples were tested. On May 7, 1813, he and Muir visited a camp of Menominee Indians near besieged Fort Meigs. "We observed them," he recalled, "seated around a large fire, over which was suspended a kettle containing their meal. Each warrior had a piece of string hanging over the edge of the vessel." At the end of each piece of string, the horrified visitors then discovered, was "a part of an American." Invited to join the Menominees, the two officers excused themselves "under the plea that we had already taken our food."

It had long been Indian practice to take scalps from enemy women and children as well as warriors. Five centuries before Thames, Indians had killed and scalped more than 400 Indian men, women, and children in a massacre at the Crow Creek site in North Dakota. This 1890 photograph shows Robert McGee, who had been scalped as a boy in Minnesota. (Library of Congress, Prints and Photographs Division)

ORDER OF BATTLE

Key:
(I) taken ill
(K) killed
(W) wounded
(NP) not present

AMERICANS AND ALLIED INDIANS (3,000)

Major-General William Henry Harrison, commander
Brigadier-General Lewis Cass, aide-de-camp
Master Commandant Oliver Hazard Perry, aide-de-camp

REGIMENT OF KENTUCKY MOUNTED INFANTRY VOLUNTEERS (960), COLONEL RICHARD M. JOHNSON (W)

1st Battalion (480), Lieutenant-Colonel James Johnson

Major DeVall Payne, second-in-command
Major James Suggett, third in command

    Company of Captain Allen A. Hamilton (45)
    Company of Captain Jacob Elliston (65)
    Company of Captain Richard Matson (90)
    Company of Captain Robert B. McAfee (140)
    Company of Captain Robert Berry (55) (W)
    Company of Captain William Church (35)
    Company of Captain John Reading (50)

2d Battalion (480), Colonel Richard M. Johnson, acting commander (W)

Major David Thompson, second-in-command

    Forlorn Hope (20): Private William Whitley, commander (K)
    Company of Captain James Coleman (85)
    Company of Captain William M. Rice (85)
    Company of Captain Samuel R. Combs (95)
    Company of Captain James Davidson (W) (95)
    Company of Captain Jacob Stucker (100)

REGIMENTS OF KENTUCKY MILITIA (1,760), MAJOR-GENERAL ISAAC SHELBY

John Adair, aide-de-camp
John J. Crittenden, aide-de-camp

Left Flank Division (two brigades) (700), Major-General Joseph Desha

4th Brigade (two regiments) (350), Colonel James Allen
    6th Regiment (five companies) (175), Colonel Richard Davenport
    8th Regiment (six companies) (175), Colonel John Callaway
5th Brigade (two regiments) (350), General Samuel Caldwell
    9th Regiment (six companies) (175), Colonel James Simrall
    10th Regiment (ten companies) (175), Colonel Philip Barbour

Center Division (three brigades) (1,050), Major-General William Henry

1st Brigade (two regiments) (350), Brigadier-General Marquis Calmes (I); Colonel George Trotter, acting commander

    1st Regiment (seven companies) (175), Colonel George Trotter (detached); Major Richard Gang, acting commander
    2d Regiment (six companies) (175), Colonel John Donaldson
2d Brigade (two regiments) (350), General David Chiles
    3d Regiment (six companies) (175), Colonel John Pogue
    4th Regiment (six companies) (175), Colonel William Mountjoy
3d Brigade (two regiments) (350), General George King
    5th Regiment (six companies) (175), Colonel Henry Renick
    7th Regiment (five companies) (175), Colonel Micah Taul (I); Major Samuel Wilson, acting commander

US ARMY UNITS (130)

US Infantry Regiment companies (120), Colonel George Paull, 27th US Infantry Regiment
24th US Infantry Company
27th US Infantry Company
2d US Artillery Regiment detachment (10), Major Eleazer Wood, US Corps of Engineers, acting commander

ALLIED INDIANS (150)

Delawares (20), John Conner and William Conner
Shawnees (65), Black Hoof and Captain Tommy
Wyandots (65), Tarhe and Between-the-Logs

BRITISH AND ALLIED INDIANS (1,350)

Major-General Henry Procter, commander

BRITISH AND CANADIANS (550)

41st Regiment of Foot (475),[1] Lieutenant-Colonel Augustus Warburton
Lieutenant-Colonel William Evans, second-in-command
Royal Regiment of Artillery (5) (one 6lb gun), Lieutenant Felix Troughton (NP); Lieutenant William Gardiner, 41st Regiment of Foot, acting commander
Canadian Light Dragoons (45), Captain Thomas Coleman
Caldwell's Rangers (25), Colonel William Caldwell

ALLIED INDIANS (800)[2]

Indian Department (10), Colonel Matthew Elliott
Indian units (790), Tecumseh (K)
Indian left wing (Creeks, Delawares, Shawnees, Potawatomis, and Wyandots) (270), Tecumseh (K)
Indian center (Ojibwes and Ottawas) (260), Winepagon (Ojibwe – K) and Naiwash (Ottawa)
Indian right wing (Fox, Kickapoos, Ojibwes, Sauks, and Winnebagos) (260), Oshawana (a.k.a. John Naudee) and Peckickee (K), Ojibwe commanders; Four Legs and Naw Kaw, Winnebago commanders

---

1 The total includes about 25 men from the 10th Royal Veteran Battalion and Royal Newfoundland Regiment of Fencible Infantry.

2 Estimates of numbers of Indians at the battle have ranged from 500 to 1,200.

OPPOSING PLANS

AMERICAN PLANS

To achieve victory on the Northwest Frontier, Harrison believed, he would have to convince the Indians that they would never receive significant British aid in war with the Americans. He also would have to defeat in battle any British and Indians who chose to fight. Before Hull's catastrophic surrender, he thought, the task would have been relatively easy. Hull's reinforced army would have swept the British from Uppermost Canada, and cut the line by which they could provide aid to the Indians. Any Indians who continued to fight could have been defeated in a small engagement like Tippecanoe.

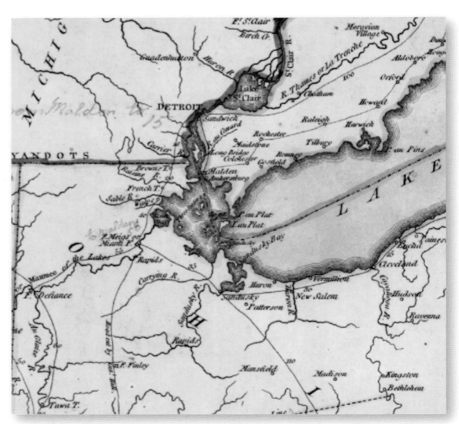

This detail from Samuel Lewis's 1812 *A Correct Map of the Seat of War* shows Harrison's area of operations. (Library of Congress, Geography and Map Division)

Harrison's lines of communication and supply.

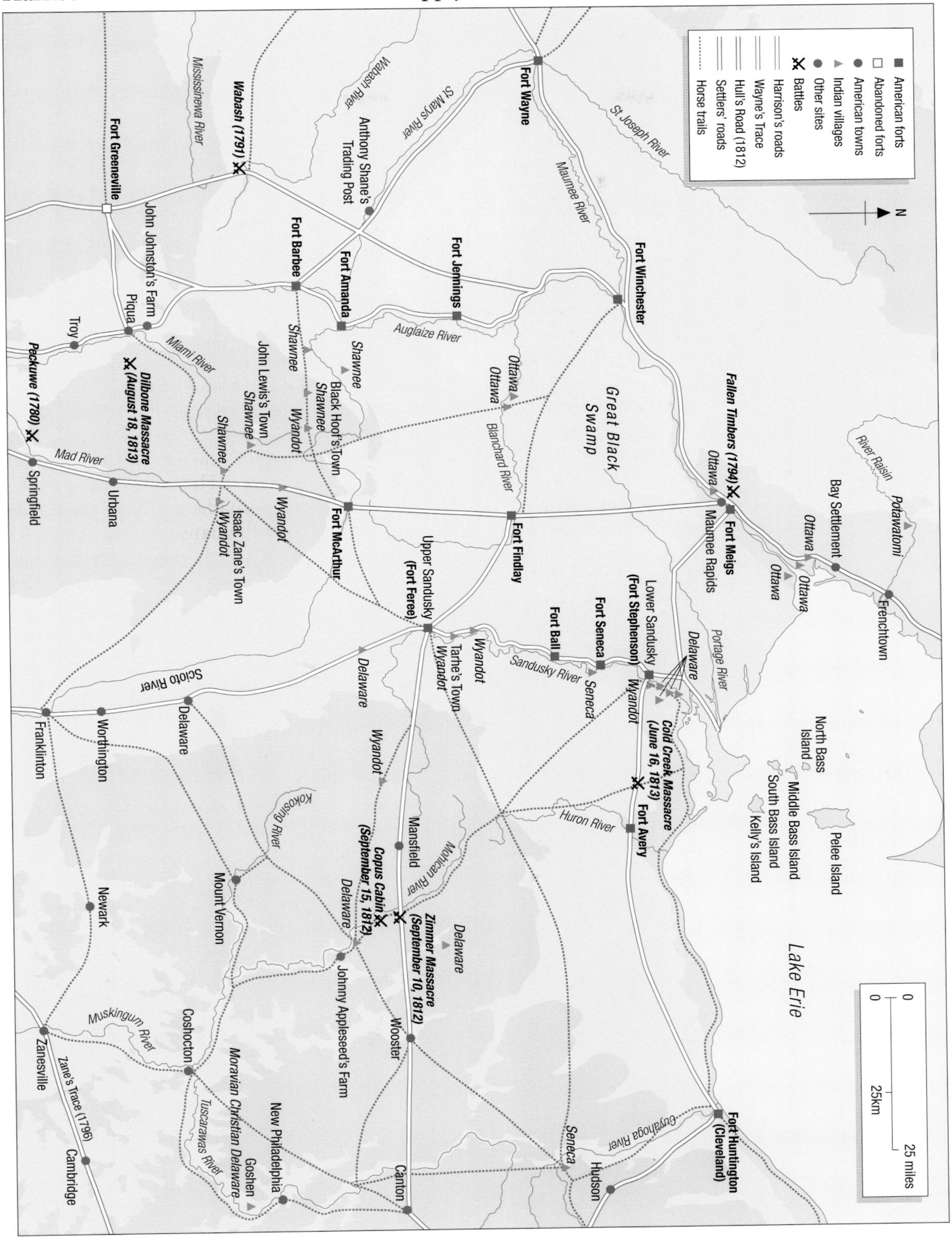

Legend:
- ■ American forts
- □ Abandoned forts
- ● American towns
- ▲ Indian villages
- ● Other sites
- ✕ Battles
- .... Settlers' roads
- Horse trails
- Hull's Road (1812)
- Wayne's Trace
- Harrison's roads

N →

Mississinewa River

Fort Greeneville

Wabash (1791) ✕

John Johnston's Farm

Anthony Shane's Trading Post

Fort Wayne

St Marys River

Wabash River

St Joseph River

Maumee River

Troy

Piqua

Peckuwe (1780) ✕

Springfield

Mad River

Urbana

Dilbone Massacre ✕ (August 18, 1813)

Miami River

Shawnee

Shawnee

John Lewis's Town

Shawnee

Shawnee

Black Hoot's Town

Fort Barbee

Fort Amanda

Fort Jennings

Auglaize River

Fort Winchester

Great Black Swamp

Ottawa

Ottawa

Blanchard River

Fort McArthur

Wyandot

Wyandot

Isaac Zane's Town

Wyandot

Upper Sandusky (Fort Feree)

Fort Findlay

Fallen Timbers (1794) ✕

Ottawa

Maumee Rapids

Fort Meigs

Bay Settlement

Ottawa

Ottawa

Ottawa

River Raisin

Potawatomi

Frenchtown

Lake Erie

North Bass Island

Middle Bass Island

South Bass Island

Kelly's Island

Pelee Island

Scioto River

Delaware

Tarhe's Town

Wyandot

Wyandot

Delaware

Sandusky River

Seneca

Fort Ball

Fort Seneca

Lower Sandusky (Fort Stephenson)

Delaware

Portage River

Wyandot

Cold Creek Massacre (June 16, 1813) ✕

Franklinton

Worthington

Kokosing River

Mount Vernon

Mansfield

Mohican River

Huron River

Fort Avery ✕

Delaware

Newark

Muskingum River

Coshocton

Moravian Christian Delaware

Johnny Appleseed's Farm

Copus Cabin ✕ (September 15, 1812)

Delaware

Zimmer Massacre ✕ (September 10, 1812)

Delaware

Wooster

Seneca

Cuyahoga River

Fort Huntington (Cleveland)

Hudson

Canton

New Philadelphia

Goshen

Tuscarawas River

Zanesville

Zane's Trace (1796)

Cambridge

0 — 25km
0 — 25 miles

Now, however, success would require recovery of Detroit and victory over a large British and Indian army in circumstances that did not favor the Americans. To defend Detroit, the British could easily transport men and supplies on Lake Erie. The Americans hoped to take control of the lake, but it was uncertain whether they would succeed. To prevail, he would have to advance by land more than 100 miles beyond the nearest American stronghold, Fort Findlay, with a large army, sufficient artillery to reduce Fort Detroit, and enough supplies to hold a fortress that might be cut off and besieged for months. The route, moreover, led through the Great Black Swamp, a morass in northwestern Ohio the size of Connecticut.

For the campaign, Harrison's soldiers would require hundreds of thousands of daily rations of meat, supplied as beef or pork, and bread, provided as flour or baked hard biscuits. Herds advancing with the army could provide the beef and pork. The flour could be moved in packhorse trains or, in larger quantities, by wagons. Wagons, however, could move only on roads, which would have to be cut. They would be pulled by thousands of horses, which, like the cattle and hogs, would themselves have to be fed. Harrison's logistical task, some would judge, was impossible. "It is," Kentucky Captain Robert McAfee would write after seeing the terrain, "beyond the power of man to feed the army by land."

But Harrison had learned as Wayne's aide the logistical principles that would control his operations. He had studied such matters as the need for alternative supply lines; the advantages and disadvantages of water and land routes; the speed at which packhorse trains and wagons could advance without killing their horses; the distance horses could carry their own food on their backs and in wagons; and how far convoys could advance before their guards consumed the food they carried. Hull's Road, Harrison concluded, must become part of a network of wagon roads that could transport supplies from different points of origin to a forwardmost base. That base, he concluded, should be at the Maumee Rapids, the site of Fallen Timbers. Behind it, there must be bases at the mouth of the Auglaize River, at Fort Findlay, and at Upper Sandusky and Lower Sandusky on the Sandusky River.

Supplies could be moved toward those bases along existing settlers' wagon roads as far as Piqua, Urbana, Franklinton, Canton, and Cleveland. From Piqua, a new road would lead to the mouth of the Auglaize, paralleling Hull's from Urbana to Fort Findlay. From Franklinton, another would lead to Lower Sandusky, and on to Upper Sandusky. From Canton, a road would be cut west to Upper Sandusky, and on to Fort Findlay; and from Cleveland

To guard his Ohio supply routes, Harrison would build Fort Winchester, at Defiance; Fort Barbee, at St Marys; Fort Amanda, near Spencerville; Fort Jennings, at Fort Jenning; Fort Feree, at Upper Sandusky; Fort Ball, at Tiffin; Fort Seneca, at Oldtown; Fort Stephenson, at Fremont; Fort Huntington, at Cleveland; Fort Avery, near Milan; and Fort Meigs, at Perrysburg. The photograph shows the appearance of the Auglaize River at the site of Fort Winchester. (Photograph by John Stanton)

The Northwest Ohio area of operations.

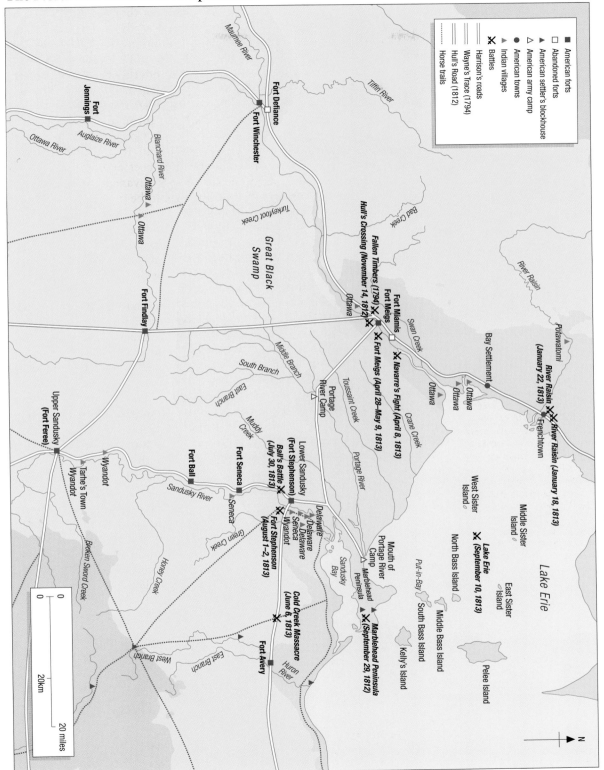

Legend:
- ■ American forts
- □ Abandoned forts
- ▶ American settler's blockhouse
- △ American army camp
- ● American towns
- ▶ Indian villages
- ✕ Battles
- ⋯ Harrison's roads
- — Wayne's Trace (1794)
- — Hull's Road (1812)
- ⋯ Horse trails

Fort Jennings
Fort Defiance
Fort Winchester
Maumee River
Tiffin River
Ottawa River
Auglaize River
Blanchard River
Ottawa
Ottawa
Turkeyfoot Creek
Great Black Swamp
Bad Creek
Hull's Crossing (November 14, 1812) ✕
Fallen Timbers (1794) ✕
Fort Miamis
Fort Meigs ■
Swan Creek
✕ Navarre's Fight (April 8, 1813)
✕ Fort Meigs (April 28–May 9, 1813)
Fort Findlay
South Branch
Middle Branch
East Branch
Muddy Creek
Portage River Camp
Toussaint Creek
Crane Creek
Ottawa
Ottawa
Ottawa
Bay Settlement
River Raisin
Potawatomi
River Raisin (January 22, 1813) ✕
✕ River Raisin (January 18, 1813)
Frenchtown ●
Upper Sandusky (Fort Feree) ■
Wyandot
Tarhe's Town
Wyandot
Fort Ball ■
Fort Seneca ■
Sandusky River
Seneca
Seneca
Green Creek
Lower Sandusky (Fort Stephenson)
Ball's Battle (July 30, 1813) ✕
Delaware
Delaware
Delaware
Seneca
Wyandot
✕ Fort Stephenson (August 1–2, 1813)
Portage River
Mouth of Portage River Camp
Marblehead Peninsula
Sandusky Bay
West Sister Island
Middle Sister Island
East Sister Island
North Bass Island
Put-in-Bay
South Bass Island
Middle Bass Island
Kelly's Island
Pelee Island
✕ Lake Erie (September 10, 1813)
✕ Marblehead Peninsula (September 29, 1812)
Lake Erie
Honey Creek
Broken Sword Creek
West Branch
East Branch
Fort Avery ■
✕ Cold Creek Massacre (June 6, 1813)
Huron River

0
0
20km
20 miles

N →

29

another would reach Lower Sandusky. Then, Hull's Road to the Maumee Rapids from Fort Findlay would be joined by others from the mouth of the Auglaize and Lower Sandusky.

When Harrison's army, artillery, and a three-month supply of food all had arrived at the Maumee Rapids, the Americans would go forward to Detroit. Then, Harrison hoped, would come the battle that would finally end the British and Indian alliance. The field would be somewhere in the Michigan Territory, he anticipated, or in Uppermost Canada, perhaps on the Thames River.

BRITISH AND INDIAN PLANS

Procter's immediate objective was to retain Detroit and the Michigan Territory. That would be possible only if Britain continued to control Lake Erie. Sufficient supplies to feed and arm a British and Indian army could not be transported to Detroit by land. It would also depend upon an effective alliance with the Indians, who alone could supply forces sufficient to defend what Brock had won.

The British commander's more ambitious goal was to establish a permanent Indian buffer state between American territory and Uppermost Canada. If he had warriors in sufficient numbers, he thought, he could invade Ohio. British and Indian victories there might force the Americans to surrender to the Indians all territory beyond the Greeneville Treaty line.

If not, Procter decided, the Indians must have at an absolute minimum the land above a line directly west from the southernmost point of Lake Erie to the Mississippi River, near what is now Muscatine, Iowa. Except for a narrow strip of land from Detroit to Frenchtown, the area taken from the Americans would be occupied only by Indians. It might be governed by Tecumseh's proposed federal union of tribes. In any case, the Indians there would be permanent allies of Britain in any future wars with the United States.

THE CAMPAIGN AND BATTLE

FROM FORT WAYNE TO THE RAISIN

What the settlers feared came on September 3, when warriors from Prophetstown attacked the Pigeon Roost settlement in the Indiana Territory. Although the settlers killed four of the raiders, the Indians killed nine adults and 15 children. The next day, 600 Potawatomis and Kickapoos attacked Fort Harrison, where 28-year-old Captain Zachary Taylor was the commandant. In desperate fighting, Taylor, who would be the 12th US President, successfully defended the fort with 25 men.

On September 5, the Sauk chief Black Hawk led 200 Sauks and Potawatomis against Fort Madison, but they failed to overcome its 36 defenders. On the same day, 600 Potawatomis and Miamis surrounded Fort Wayne. At their head were Winamac and Five Medals. The Potawatomi chiefs, who had opposed Tecumseh's efforts to unite the Indians, now had concluded that the Americans were going to lose the war. Winamac urged the fort's frightened commandant to surrender to avoid a massacre. Captain James Rhea, a Wabash survivor, agreed. But his officers mutinied, and besieged Fort Wayne held out.

Although the Shawnee tribe remained neutral, many individual warriors offered to aid the Americans. During the siege of Fort Wayne, Tecumseh's daring nephew Johnny Logan (Spemica Lawba) crept through the surrounding Indians to reassure the soldiers and settlers that help was on its way. At a November 22, 1812 skirmish of Indian scouts, he killed Winamac. Mortally wounded in the engagement, the Shawnee was buried with the honors of an American officer at the mouth of the Auglaize River. (Photograph by Dale Benington)

By September 9, Russell was marching from Vincennes to relieve Fort Harrison with a force of 1,000 US Army Rangers, 7th Infantry soldiers from Fort Knox, and Indiana Territory militiamen. Harrison was advancing from Wayne's abandoned Fort St Marys toward the trading post of the Shawnee Anthony Shane, where Adams's Ohioans were waiting.

On September 12, Russell's and Harrison's columns reached the forts. But their arrival did not end the danger. On September 13, Indians killed at the Narrows 11 men guarding a convoy advancing to Fort Harrison. Two days later, they killed seven with another convoy.

On September 14, British Captain Adam Muir left Fort Malden with 50 regulars, 150 militiamen, and three pieces of artillery to capture Fort Wayne. In the absence of the wounded Tecumseh, who had returned to Prophetstown, Roundhead led the 800 Indians with him. That same day, Harrison commenced a series of retaliatory operations against the Indian villages nearest the fort. Wells led his, Scott's, and Johnson's regiments against Five Medals' Town, and Payne marched with Allen's, Lewis's, and Garrard's units against Miami villages on the Wabash. On September 16, Findlay's Ohioans advanced from St Marys to destroy the towns of the Blanchard River Ottawas. Simrall's dragoons, dispatched to burn Miami villages on the Eel River, overpowered a force of Miami defenders at the September 19 battle of the Eel River.

When Winchester arrived in Fort Wayne, Harrison recommended that the still senior Tennessean lead the American forces there down the Maumee to the mouth of the Auglaize River. At the same time, he would march with Barbee's, Jennings's, Pogue's, and Tupper's men down the Auglaize to join him. On September 24, as Winchester's army was moving down the Maumee, a welcome message from Eustis reached Harrison in Piqua. He, not Winchester, would command the Americans on the Northwest Frontier.

On September 25, Muir's scouts met Winchester's just west of the mouth of the Auglaize. When a prisoner reported that there were nearly 3,000 Americans, the alarmed British commander halted his advance. Muir then learned how difficult it would be to fulfill Brock's plan to use the Indians against the Americans.

During the next three days, 500 of his warriors disappeared. About 130 of them had left to go raiding in Ohio. On September 29, they encountered 65 of Perkins's Ohio militiamen on the Marblehead Peninsula. In 12 hours of scattered fighting, 8 Ohioans fell, and about 20 of the Indian raiders.

The 300 warriors who remained with Muir demanded a battle. Two shamans, they said, had dreamed that they would defeat the Americans. If they failed, Roundhead told Muir, they could just disappear into the woods. His men and guns could not, the British captain testily replied before ordering a retreat. After advancing to the mouth of the Auglaize, Winchester then began building near the site of Wayne's abandoned Fort Defiance what would be called Fort Winchester.

During the two years that followed Pigeon Roost, Indian raiders killed or captured about 100 settlers. The principal attacks in Ohio were the September 10, 1812 Zimmer Massacre near Perrysville; the September 15, 1812 battle at the nearby Copus Cabin; the June 6, 1813 Cold Creek Massacre at Castalia; and the August 18, 1813 Dilbone Massacre near Piqua. After the Zimmer Massacre, the Swedenborgian missionary John Chapman, known for his planting of apple trees as "Johnny Appleseed," ran 30 miles from his nearby farm to summon militiamen from Mount Vernon. This engraving in the 1889 edition of Henry Howe's *Historical Collections of Ohio* preserved a sketch of Johnny Appleseed by his friend Rosella Price. (Author's collection)

When the frustrated Muir reached Malden, he found that a gloomy Procter had had his own glimpse of problems to come. To reconcile the Michigan Territory settlers to their new status as British subjects, Procter had planned to announce that his government would punish as thieves any Indians who took their property. But Brock had objected "in a most forceful manner." All that could be done, Procter was told, was to try to persuade the Indian chiefs to restrain their warriors.

The capacity of the Indians to raid American settlements, Harrison thought, could be reduced by driving them farther and farther from settled areas. He now ordered expeditions against more distant towns. The most ambitious was a coordinated attack by two forces on Kickapoo and Potawatomi villages on the Illinois River. On October 14, Kentucky Brigadier-General Samuel Hopkins led 2,000 Kentuckians from Fort Harrison. On October 18, Russell and 300 men rode north from Fort Russell, his base near St Louis, to meet them. Russell's men burned several villages and killed 25 defenders. But Hopkins's men lost their way. After exhausting their food, and narrowly escaping a prairie fire set by Indians, they returned to Fort Harrison.

In Ohio, Harrison's plans were proceeding more smoothly. Lieutenant-Colonel James Ball's 2d US Dragoon Regiment squadron soon would arrive. Brigadier-General George Crooks was coming with 1,000 militiamen from western Pennsylvania, and Brigadier-General Joel Leftwich with 1,200 from western Virginia. When they joined his army, Harrison would have about 7,000 men until the six-month terms of his Kentucky and Ohio militiamen began to expire in February, and those of his Pennsylvanians and Virginians in March. He also would have the guns needed to recover Detroit. Twenty-one, he was told, were on their way from Pittsburgh.

The American commander also would have everything his army would need. Its principal contractor, Ebenezer Denny, who had been an aide to General Arthur St Clair at Wabash, was forwarding from Pittsburgh supplies for a campaign that would last at least 90 days. Harrison, who knew what his men would face when winter arrived, also had appealed to the women of Kentucky and Ohio to supplement the army's stores of warm clothing and blankets. Provided with cloth from the army's stores, the ladies of Dayton now were at work on a project to provide 1,800 wool shirts.

The American commander, moreover, soon would be able to move his men, guns, and supplies forward toward Detroit on a network of wagon

After the siege of Fort Wayne, the Americans built a more formidable fortress to replace Wayne's 1794 stronghold. This reproduction of the new fort stands in Fort Wayne's Old Fort Park. (Photograph by John Stanton)

roads. Before returning to Kentucky, Barbee's, Jennings's, and Pogue's men were completing a supply road from Piqua to Fort Winchester. More than 2,000 Ohio militiamen, led by brigadier-generals Simon Perkins and Reasin Beall, were cutting others from Franklinton, Canton, and Cleveland toward Upper and Lower Sandusky, and on to Fort Findlay and the Maumee Rapids.

When the roads were completed, and the artillery and supplies ready, Winchester would lead the regiments of Wells, Allen, Lewis, and Scott from Fort Winchester to the Maumee Rapids. Tupper's Ohioans would join them from Fort Findlay; Leftwich's Virginians and Crooks's Pennsylvanians from Upper Sandusky; and Perkins and another 600 Ohioans from Lower Sandusky. By the end of November, Harrison thought, his men, guns, and supplies would be at the rapids, ready to advance to Detroit.

But on October 28, a heavy rain began to beat on the windows of the American commander's headquarters in Franklinton. The relentless downpour, which continued for nearly an entire month, created almost impossible conditions for the luckless men building roads, transporting supplies, and advancing to forward bases. The water, wrote one of Leftwich's Virginians "in 8 miles of the best of the road took us over the knees and often to the middle. In this swamp you lose sight of terra firma altogether … When we went to sleep, it was on two logs laid close together to keep our bodies from the damp ground. The loftiest spirit that ever inhabited the human breast would have been tamed amid the difficulties that surrounded us."

The conditions on the roads, moreover, accelerated the rate at which men and horses consumed the rations their convoys carried. A wagon carrying flour from Chillicothe to Upper Sandusky, Harrison reported to Eustis, now had to be accompanied by two more, filled with food for the three wagons' horse teams.

At his headquarters in Amherstburg, Procter had his own logistical problem. The families of Indian warriors depended upon the game the warriors killed. To make service with the British more attractive, Elliott and Dickson had urged warriors to bring their women and children, who would be fed at Detroit and Malden while they battled the Americans. Now the numbers had begun to exceed the capacity of the British Indian welfare program to provide food.

On November 7, Elliott led a force of 75 British regulars and 400 Indians to recover unharvested corn in abandoned fields on the Maumee River. When Tupper learned that they were at the rapids, he led 650 men from Fort Findlay to drive them back from Ohio. On November 14, Tupper's men met Elliott's at Hull's Crossing on the Maumee. The Americans killed eight before the British and Indians fled.

Harrison probably used this 1807 house as his headquarters in Franklinton, now Columbus. (Photograph by Dale Benington)

As Tupper's men were returning to Fort Findlay, Hopkins was conducting another operation against the Indians. On November 10, he led 1,250 Kentucky horsemen against Prophetstown and other villages on the Wabash. Although they burned the Prophet's village and two nearby towns, the Indians killed 16 in a November 22 ambush at Wildcat Creek.

The interior of the reconstructed council house at the site of Prophetstown. (Photograph by Erin Worthy)

That same day, Harrison dispatched from Franklinton 600 horsemen for the last of the year's operations against the Indians, an attack on villages near the mouth of the Mississinewa River. Lieutenant-Colonel John Campbell led west toward Wayne's abandoned Fort Greeneville mounted infantrymen from his 19th US Infantry Regiment, Ball's 2d US Dragoon squadron, and Simrall's and Garrard's Kentucky dragoons. With them went the Pittsburgh Blues, a 100-man unit of Crooks's Pennsylvanians led by Captain James Butler, the son of the famous Brigadier-General Richard Butler, who had died at Wabash.

As Campbell's men rode toward Greenville Creek, the rain turned to snow, which accumulated to a depth of 2ft. The blizzard, which forced Hopkins to return to Vincennes, almost completely halted Harrison's movement of supplies. Now, he was told, wagons could advance only a half mile a day from Piqua. Two trips from Urbana to Fort McArthur, he wrote to Eustis, "will completely destroy a brigade of packhorses." The desperate American commander ordered the construction of a fleet of sleds to transport his supplies.

On December 10, Lieutenant Levi Hukill of the 1st US Light Dragoon Regiment finally reached Upper Sandusky with the first guns of the army's long-awaited artillery. When Harrison learned of the arrival, he moved his headquarters to Upper Sandusky. The weather then turned much colder. A thick cover of ice formed over the snow.

The cemetery at Fort Amanda State Memorial. (Photograph by Dale Benington)

The conditions on the roads defied description. Their courses, an American officer remembered, could be seen in the sky as rows of buzzards awaiting more dead horses. But it was worse at Harrison's advanced forts and camps. There men had begun dying from disease, starvation, and hypothermia. The Americans dug the graves in mud; then in snow; and finally down through the ice. By the end of December, they numbered more than 500.

The ice, however, allowed Campbell's men to reach Fort Greeneville on December 14. "Had it been otherwise," said Private John Niebaum of Butler's Pittsburgh Blues, "the difficulties from the number of creeks and the great swamps we had to cross would have rendered it impossible." They found waiting beside the decaying fort's ice-covered walls 96 Kentucky horsemen. Major John Adair had led them up Wayne's old trace, past the site of the November 6, 1792 battle of Fort St Clair, where he had led the Kentuckians against the Indians 20 years before. Adair's men were to follow Campbell's, and await them with provisions they could eat on their return.

Led by Shane, the Michigan Territory scout James Knaggs, and the Delaware trader William Conner, Campbell's men then rode toward the mouth of the Mississinewa. On December 17, they destroyed three villages, killing eight warriors and taking 42 prisoners without any loss. But an hour before daybreak on December 18, 300 hastily assembled warriors surrounded the American camp. A sentinel, remembered Private Nathaniel Vernon of the Blues, called out: "'Who comes there?' 'Potawatomi, God damn you,' was the reply in good English, with a shot aimed at him."

For a while, the Indians threatened to break through the American perimeter. But when the sun finally rose, a charge by Captain George Trotter's troop of Simrall's dragoons sent the warriors fleeing from the field. At cost of 12 dead and 46 wounded, the Americans killed over 30 Indians, and wounded still more.

The Americans' ammunition and food, however, were almost exhausted. The retreat was an ordeal of cold and hunger. "At every halt," Vernon remembered, "the sock would freeze next to the foot; and so remain, until the friction of the foot and the moccasin would again thaw it." On December 23, the starving Americans reached Adair's waiting men and packhorses. By then, Vernon remembered, 350 of the men, including Garrard, were disabled by frostbite.

The weather, thought the indomitable American commander, had delayed his campaign, but had not defeated him. Sleds atop the ice were again moving his artillery and supplies forward. On the day Campbell's starving men reached Adair's food, a long-awaited flour convoy arrived at Fort Winchester. On December 30, Winchester finally led toward the Maumee Rapids Colonel Samuel Wells's 17th US Infantry and Allen's, Lewis's, and Scott's Kentucky regiments.

On January 16, the American commander learned at Lower Sandusky that Winchester had reached the rapids. He and Perkins's 600 men then went forward to join him. That evening, Winchester met with his officers to decide whether to advance to Frenchtown, a two-day march ahead. Harrison had not authorized an advance to the town, but settlers from Frenchtown had reported that Indians there were threatening to kill them.

After cutting their roads through a nightmare of dirt, water, mud, snow, and ice, Perkins's and Beall's Ohio militiamen crowned their effort with an almost superhuman achievement. To complete the road from Lower Sandusky to the Maumee Rapids, they built a 15-mile-long log causeway through the most difficult area of the Great Black Swamp. Beall's 1815 house in Wooster, Ohio, is now a museum. (Courtesy of the Wayne County Historical Society and Museum)

Wells objected to the advance. The 58-year-old frontiersman had fought Indians at Point Pleasant and during the Revolutionary War, survived Wabash, and led Kentucky horsemen at Fallen Timbers and Tippecanoe. Frenchtown, he said, was too close to Fort Malden, only 20 miles away across the frozen Detroit River. But Winchester and the Kentucky regiment commanders agreed that the army should go forward to protect the settlers.

On January 17, the American scout Peter Navarre, whose father had founded Frenchtown, led the 650 men in Allen's and Lewis's regiments toward the village. The following day, they reached the 70-yard-wide River Raisin. Across the river, at Frenchtown, they found 200 Potawatomis, 75 Canadian militiamen, and a 3lb gun. Aided by 100 local settlers, they drove the Indians and Canadians from the settlement. The cost was 12 dead and 55 wounded.

When Winchester received news of the victory, he left Scott's 300-man regiment at the Maumee Rapids and advanced toward Frenchtown with Wells and his 300 men. They arrived late on January 20. On the same evening, Harrison reached the rapids.

When Wells inspected the positions in Frenchtown on January 21, he did not like what he saw. To the north, which the Americans faced, and to the east and west, a 5ft-high picket fence extended around the town. Lewis's regiment, on the left, was in the town, to the east and south of the fence. Allen's was to Lewis's right, south of the fence and further east beyond the town. Wells's own regiment, to the right of Allen's, was in an open field. The army's store of ammunition, moreover, was at Winchester's headquarters, almost a mile behind the town.

Wells urged Winchester to fortify the position, distribute the army's ammunition, and send scouts out as far as Brownstown. That, Winchester replied, could wait until the following day. A settler, Navarre then reported, had seen a force of British and Indians crossing the Detroit River. That, Winchester responded, was just "conjecture."

Wells then learned that Harrison had reached the rapids. On the pretense of escorting an advancing supply convoy, he rode all night to share his concerns with the American commander. By noon on January 22, an alarmed

Cragfont, James Winchester's 1805 house, is now a museum in Castalian Springs, Tennessee. (Library of Congress, Prints and Photographs Division)

Harrison was marching toward Frenchtown with Wells, Scott's 300 men, and Perkins's 600. But it was too late.

At 6.00am on January 22, 600 British regulars and Canadian militiamen, and six 3lb guns, were on the ground to the north of the town. Some 800 warriors, led by Roundhead, were in a curving line to their left, ahead of and flanking the American 17th Infantry. The guns concentrated their fire on the exposed American regulars, annihilating them with shells and canister shot. As Allen and Lewis led companies to support the beleaguered 17th Regiment soldiers, Roundhead's Indians attacked. Sweeping Allen, Lewis, and their companies with them, the surviving regulars fled toward safety across the River Raisin.

Led by Major George Madison of Lewis's regiment, the 500 remaining Kentuckians fought on behind the Frenchtown fence. Madison, who had been wounded at Wabash, and served as Adair's second-in-command at Fort St Clair, had his riflemen silence the British guns. Procter then ordered his regulars to fix their bayonets. In three disastrous charges, half fell killed or wounded by the Kentuckians' rifle balls.

The frustrated British commander, who had 23 dead and 161 wounded, then received a false report that Harrison and 1,000 men were only 8 miles away. But before Procter could order a retreat, Roundhead arrived with Winchester, whom the Indians had captured. The British commander told him, Winchester remembered, that unless the Kentuckians surrendered

The painter Mathew Jouett fought at the Raisin as a private in the regiment of his friend Colonel John Allen, who fell at the battle. In 1814, he painted this portrait of Allen from memory for the fallen commander's family. (Courtesy of the Allen County Courthouse Preservation Trust)

"The snow," wrote Captain James Price of Lewis's regiment when he arrived at Frenchtown on January 18, "is two feet deep. The crust is very hard and we walk over it and ride upon it by horseback." This split-rail fence now traces the line of the picket fence defended by the Kentuckians on January 22. (US National Park Service, Staff Photograph)

immediately, "no responsibility would be taken for the conduct of the savages."

By 10.00am, Madison's men each had only two or three balls left. Procter, the Kentucky major recalled, appeared with one of Winchester's aides, and demanded "with great haughtiness" that Madison comply with an order from Winchester to surrender. He would not, the Kentuckian replied, unless Procter promised that British soldiers would guard the American prisoners and wounded until they were taken to Fort Malden. The British commander then agreed to Madison's terms.

Navarre, who escaped, reached Harrison's advancing reinforcements and reported that Winchester's army had been destroyed. The American commander led his force back to the rapids and on toward Lower Sandusky. After halting at a camp on the Portage River, he ordered Tupper's, Crooks's, and Leftwich's men, and his artillery, forward toward the Maumee Rapids.

By February 6, Harrison had at the rapids 3,500 men and 22 guns. But time had nearly run out. In nine days, the enlistment terms of Scott's, Tupper's, and Perkins's men would expire. A hard rain then began to melt the ice. For five days, Harrison waited for the ground to freeze again. When it did, he hoped, he would by a dramatic plea persuade the militiamen to march forward with him to Detroit.

This 1907 Nicola Marschall portrait depicts George Madison, who would be elected governor of Kentucky in 1816. (Kentucky Historical Society, 1908.25)

But the downpour continued. On February 11, the disappointed American commander wrote to Secretary of War John Armstrong, who had replaced Eustis: "I have waited with an anxiety which I cannot describe for a change in the weather, and until this day I never abandoned the hope of being able to execute the plan which I had formed."

Detroit was still British. But the American commander had built the logistical network needed to recover and hold it. Harrison ordered Captain Eleazer Wood of the US Army Corps of Engineers to build at the Maumee Rapids a massive stronghold, 2,500 yards in circumference. From what would be called Fort Meigs, the American commander vowed, he would resume the campaign in June.

FROM THE RAISIN TO FORT STEPHENSON

When Procter returned to Amherstburg, he learned that Brock's letter to the Earl of Liverpool had produced results. "I entirely concur," Earl Bathurst, the new Minister for War and the Colonies, had written to Prévost, "as to the necessity of securing the territories of the Indians from encroachment … Whenever negotiations for peace may be entered into, the security of their possessions may not be either compromised or forgotten."

Prévost now was to send him reinforcements. The rest of the 41st was on its way and also 100 men of the Royal Newfoundland Regiment of Fencible

Infantry. He also was to have many more Indians. To attract them, the British would offer disability payments for the seriously wounded, and death benefits for the families of those who fell. In addition, chiefs and warriors would receive shares of the prize money that would come from the taking of the rich American towns.

In the spring, Procter decided, he would invade Ohio with thousands of soldiers and warriors, and ample artillery. His regulars and warriors would sweep away the American militiamen. His guns would quickly reduce the Americans' wooden forts. By the end of 1813, perhaps, the Union Jack would fly over Chillicothe, the Ohio capital.

For his victory at the Raisin, Procter would be promoted to brigadier-, and then major-general. But beneath the glow of the British commander's glory, more of the price of fulfilling Brock's plan had appeared in ugly form. At Frenchtown, remembered Lieutenant William Caldwell of Lewis's regiment, the Indians killed "more than twenty of our soldiers after we had surrendered." They'd also claimed 45 of the 483 American prisoners, many of whom were never seen again.

Procter, moreover, had left 60 wounded Americans unguarded in houses in Frenchtown. When Indians found them on January 23, they set the houses afire. "I saw," recalled Private Elias Darnell of Lewis's regiment, "my fellow soldiers, naked and wounded, crawling out of the houses to avoid being consumed by the flames." Those who escaped were tomahawked if they could not walk.

"It is impossible," Procter said dismissively, "to save any prisoner and the attempt has endangered the lives of several of our people where the Indians have lost their lives." But it was one thing, his embarrassed officers and men thought, to threaten timid American commanders, and another to burn wounded American prisoners alive. The Indians, wrote a horrified British officer, were "monsters in human shape." There was, remembered the Canadian commissary Robert Reynolds, "intense feeling in our camp. Procter was greatly blamed by us."

The Michigan Territory settlers, moreover, were on the brink of rebellion. Procter arrested four found among the Raisin prisoners, and another 29 in Detroit on suspicion of planning an uprising. Michigan, he announced, now would be under martial law. And every settler must take an oath of loyalty to the crown. "Any pretense at a benevolent occupation," wrote Augustus Woodward, who had been the territory's chief justice, "was ended."

The Indians then began taking from the terrified Michigan settlers anything they fancied. Private Shadrach Byfield

The 1784 house of Peter Navarre's father survives as a museum in Frenchtown, now Monroe, Michigan. (Author's collection)

of the 41st had made friends with an American family who lived in a fine house near Detroit. When he next saw them, he remembered, they were living "in a cottage reduced to a state of extreme poverty. The Indians had deprived them of all their property."

On March 6, Harrison left Fort Meigs for Cincinnati, where he would plan his spring campaign. Released from captivity, Cass and McArthur would join his army as US Army brigadier-generals. Cass would command Ball's dragoons, Owings's 24th US Infantry Regiment, and Paull's 27th. McArthur would have the 17th, which Wells was rebuilding; John Miller's 19th, and Anderson's 28th.

A large militia force, moreover, would supplement Harrison's nearly 2,000 regulars. To replace Tupper's and Perkins's Ohioans, Crooks's Pennsylvanians, and Leftwich's Virginians, Brigadier-General John Wingate had raised two new Ohio regiments. To replace Allen's, Lewis's, and Scott's men, Major-General Green Clay was bringing two new Kentucky regiments, led by lieutenant-colonels William Boswell and William Dudley. To replace Garrard's and Simrall's frostbitten dragoons, who had disbanded after Mississinewa, Richard M. Johnson was recruiting a regiment of Kentucky mounted riflemen like those he had led to Fort Wayne in 1812. When Johnson's men reached Fort Meigs in early June, Harrison would march up Hull's Road.

In Cincinnati, however, the American commander received new instructions from Armstrong. He was not to march to Detroit, the Secretary of War ordered. After an American fleet had taken control of Lake Erie, he was to sail to Detroit with Cass's and McArthur's brigades; and he was not, Armstrong said, to use any more Kentucky militia units in the war.

But Armstrong's promised fleet, a discouraged Harrison thought, might fail to win control of the lake. Without militia support, his promised army of newly recruited regulars might be too small to defeat a much larger British and Indian army. Another year then would end like 1812, with the Michigan Territory still British.

Alarming news from Fort Meigs then distracted the American commander from his depression. A British and Indian army, Wood reported, was assembling to attack the fort. Wingate's Ohioans had not arrived to replace the departing men of Crooks and Leftwich. Butler's Pittsburgh Blues, and a few other companies, had agreed to remain beyond their enlistment terms. But soon he might have to defend the fort only a few hundred men.

Fort Meigs, which had seven blockhouses, 15ft-high timber walls, and high earthen ramparts, has been reconstructed on its original site in Maumee, Ohio. This gun at the fort is aimed at the high ground across the Maumee River occupied by the British artillery. (Photograph by Dale Benington)

The American commander left Cincinnati immediately with three companies of Boswell's regiment. The rest of Clay's men, he ordered, were to march to Fort Winchester. Wingate's regiments, Miller's 19th Regiment, and Ball's dragoons were to advance to Fort Meigs at once.

As Harrison rode north, Indians began appearing in the woods around Wood's fort. On April 8, 15 warriors killed a soldier and captured two others. Navarre and 11 other scouts then pursued the Indians 6 miles down the Maumee. At Navarre's Fight, they killed five of the raiders and wounded three, at a cost of two dead and three wounded. When Harrison arrived four days later, reinforcements had swollen the garrison to about 1,600.

In Amherstburg, chiefs like the famous Sauk commander Black Hawk were arriving daily, bringing for the invasion bands of Dakotas and Fox, Kickapoos and Menominees, Ottawas and Ojibwes, Potawatomis, Sauks, and Winnebagos. On April 16, the Indian for whom Procter had been waiting appeared. A few days' march behind him, Tecumseh told the British commander, hundreds more warriors were coming.

Although Indians were still arriving on April 23, the invasion of Ohio commenced. Tecumseh led 1,300 warriors down Hull's Road. A British fleet carried across Lake Erie 533 British regulars, 462 Canadian militiamen, Hull's two 24lb guns from Detroit, and eight smaller pieces. The *Eliza* and *General Myers*, gunboats that could sail up the Maumee, carried still more ordnance.

This colored lithograph in McKenney and Hall's 1848 *History of the Indian Tribes of North America* reproduced an 1837 Charles Bird King portrait of Black Hawk. (Author's collection)

When the American commander learned on April 27 that the invaders had reached the Maumee, he sent messengers to Clay, ordering him to advance from Fort Winchester, and to Cass, McArthur, and Meigs, urging them to send reinforcements as soon as possible. Harrison, who had little ammunition for his own guns, was especially troubled by the prospect of a massive artillery bombardment.

Soon Harrison's officers and men were working around the clock in eight-hour shifts. They dug two large underground magazines for the fort's ammunition; they covered all roofs with dirt to retard fire; and they piled up two great mounds, 12ft high, 20ft wide, and 300 yards long. Behind the massive traverses, which ran the length of the fort, the Americans would huddle while the enemy guns across the river fired.

On May 1 and May 2, the sky rained metal on Fort Meigs. But the bombardment had no effect beyond killing six Americans, wounding 11, and damaging several of the blockhouse roofs. On May 3, Procter increased the rate of fire, but it still did little damage. Tecumseh, who was beside himself with frustration, sent a message to Harrison. "Come out," the Shawnee said, "and give me battle. You talked like a brave when we met at Vincennes, and I respected you. But now you hide behind logs and in the earth like a groundhog."

To evade the effect of Harrison's traverses, Procter sent men across the river to construct a battery of three guns east of the fort. Their shells, which would fly on paths paralleling the traverses, would scour the ground where the Americans hid.

After a brief barrage from the new position on April 4, Procter sent a message to Harrison. Only an American surrender, he said, would avoid a massacre by the Indians when the fort was taken. "Tell General Procter," Harrison responded, "that if he shall take the fort it will be under circumstances that will do him more honor than a thousand surrenders."

By the time British shells began falling again, the Americans were busy with their shovels. They built 12 traverses perpendicular to those they already had dug. By the end of the day, they had shelter from fire from the new direction.

That night, a messenger from Clay arrived. Traveling down the Maumee in pirogues, his Kentuckians had reached a site only two hours up the river. The delighted American commander then planned a complex operation for April 5. Colonel John Miller would lead his 275 regulars, and Captain William Sebree's 75-man company of Boswell's regiment, against the three British guns on the fort side of the Maumee. Dudley's 700 men would spike the British artillery across the river, and retreat to the fort. Boswell's 400 would land on the fort side of the river and fight their way through the Indians to join Harrison.

At first the plan worked smoothly. Miller's men attacked the three guns east of the fort, which were defended by Lieutenant Richard Bullock's 130 British regulars, and 300 Indians led by Tecumseh. After a fierce battle, in which the Americans lost 30 killed and 90 wounded, they overpowered the defenders, spiked the guns, and returned to the fort with 42 prisoners. Boswell's men, aided by Butler's Pittsburgh Blues, also reached the fort safely.

Captain William Sebree drew this map of the Fort Meigs area. The added names indicate the Maumee River flowing from left to right around two large islands, past Fort Meigs and abandoned British Fort Miamis. The added numbers show the sites of: 1. the battle of Fallen Timbers; 2. the landing of Dudley's regiment; 3. the landing of Boswell's regiment; 4. the attack of Dudley's regiment on British artillery; 5. the attack of the Indians on Dudley's regiment; 6. the massacre of captured Americans; 7. the attack of Colonel John Miller's force on British artillery; and 8. the July 26, 1813 sham battle of the British and Indians. (Library of Congress, Geography and Map Division)

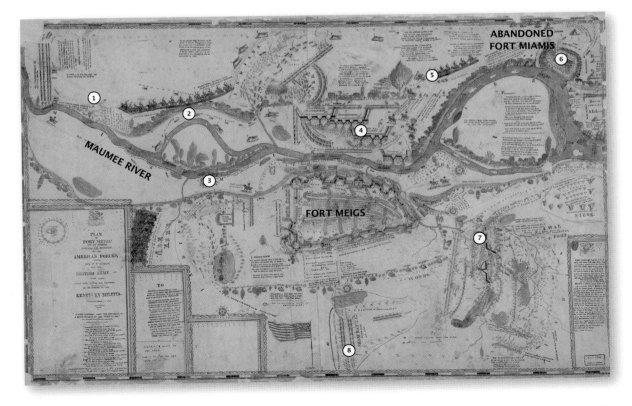

But Dudley's men, after completing their assignment, pursued the British and Indian defenders until they were battling three times their number. At what would be remembered as Dudley's Defeat, the Kentucky commander and 50 of his men fell, and almost 100 were wounded. When 635 surrendered, they were imprisoned within the decaying walls of old British Fort Miamis, only 100 yards from Procter's headquarters tent.

Soon the Ottawa chief Split Nose arrived with warriors to attack the captured Americans. One of the 50 British regulars guarding the prisoners tried to protect them. "An old and excellent soldier named Russell, of the 41st," recalled Richardson, "was shot through the heart while endeavoring to wrest a victim from the grasp of his murderer."

Procter and his officers watched what followed in stunned silence. Before Tecumseh arrived and halted the proceedings, Split Nose's warriors killed nearly 40 American prisoners. The Ottawa, said an appalled John Norton, was "a worthless chief," and the men he led "wretches."

But the warriors who killed Russell and the prisoners went unpunished, and no one tried to stop what followed. The Indians chose from among the massacre survivors the Americans they would keep. "I saw Corporal Smith of our company bidding farewell to his friends, and pointing to the Indian with whom he was to go," remembered Lieutenant Joseph Underwood, "I never heard of his return."

To Procter's relief, a white flag then appeared above Fort Meigs. The defeat of Dudley's men, the elated British commander briefly thought, had been the final blow. But when Harrison's herald arrived, he brought not an offer to surrender, but a proposal to exchange prisoners.

Procter's hopes of capturing the American stronghold then vanished like a wafting cloud of smoke. After firing 1,676 rounds, his guns had nearly exhausted their ammunition. Cass, McArthur, and 2,000 Americans, his scouts reported, were coming on the road from Fort Findlay. Meigs and another thousand were marching from Lower Sandusky. Procter's militiamen refused to stay any longer, and his Indians began to disappear. By May 8, the crestfallen British commander remembered, "I was left with Tecumseh and less than 20 chiefs and warriors." The next day, the British Army sailed back to Amherstburg.

On May 26, Richard M. Johnson's regiment crossed the Ohio River. Born to fight, Johnson had come under fire at an early age. During the 1782 siege of Bryan Station, one of Girty's Indians had fired a flaming arrow into the 2-year-old Kentuckian's crib. Twelve hundred horsemen had responded to the popular commander's call for volunteers.

On June 8, Harrison sent Johnson's riders on the first of the year's raids on Indian villages, against Five Medals' Town on the St Joseph River. Three days later, Colonel Joseph Bartholomew, who had fought at Tippecanoe, led 150 Indiana Territory militiamen against

This marker in Maumee, Ohio, honors 41st Regiment of Foot Private Patrick Russell, who fell 4,000 miles from his Irish home trying to protect American prisoners. (Photograph by Dale Benington)

villages on the White River. The Indian towns, Johnson and Bartholomew reported, were all abandoned.

Constrained by Armstrong's orders, the American commander could do little but wait for construction of the American fleet. Alarmed at the project, the British had begun building at Amherstburg the warship *Detroit*, a vessel that could equal the power of the *Queen Charlotte*. On June 16, an experienced Royal Navy officer arrived to supervise defense of the lake. Commander Robert Barclay was only 27, but he had fought at Trafalgar in 1805, and lost his left arm capturing a French frigate in 1809.

News that the Ohio Delawares, Shawnees, and Wyandots had decided to fight with the Americans briefly relieved Harrison's frustration. On June 21, their chiefs met with the American commander in Franklinton. He received from them, reported the Franklinton *Freeman's Chronicle* on June 24, a promise that their warriors would not "kill or injure old men, women, children nor prisoners."

Eyes that American militiamen could not match soon were searching the Ohio woods for signs of raiders. A Delaware killed one of Tecumseh's Indians, who said that he had come to Ohio to assassinate the American commander. The Shawnee Captain Johnny, a son of the famous female chief Nonhelema, and nephew of Cornstalk, the Shawnee commander at Point Pleasant, volunteered to guard Harrison's tent every night for the rest of the campaign.

Russell then led the last of the year's expeditions against the Indians. On July 1,600 US Army Rangers and Indiana Territory militiamen began a 500-mile-long ride up the White River East Fork and down the Wabash. But Russell too found only abandoned villages.

The Indians who had lived in the villages had joined thousands of others in a migration to camps near Detroit and Amherstburg. Soon the warriors and their families outnumbered the settlers in the Michigan Territory and Uppermost Canada. They were consuming, Elliott's British Indian Department calculated in July, 14,000 daily rations.

Procter now had 3,500 warriors eager for battle, but he had no interest in using them to invade Ohio again. If an American fleet took control of Lake Erie, he thought, he might be cut off in Ohio, unable to retreat.

Tecumseh used his great power as an orator to urge the bored warriors to remain – but finally, the Shawnee threatened to leave himself. He had devised a plan to capture Fort Meigs, Tecumseh told the British commander, and unless the British returned to Ohio, their alliance with the Indians would end. Procter reluctantly agreed to another invasion.

This boulder in Columbus marks the site of the June 21, 1813 Franklinton council. (Dale Benington)

The American commander passed the time inspecting the forts that guarded Ohio from invasion. In addition to Fort Meigs, there was Fort Stephenson on the Sandusky River, commanded by 21-year-old Major George Croghan of the 17th US Infantry; and also Fort Huntington, where boats to carry American soldiers to Canada were being built on the Cuyahoga River. Finally, Harrison could tolerate the waiting no longer. If the Americans failed to take control of Lake Erie, he decided, he nonetheless would recover Detroit by land.

The American commander then took action that he knew would infuriate Armstrong. In a July 20 letter to Shelby, Harrison asked the Kentucky governor to send him 3,000 more mounted riflemen; and he added a suggestion that, he thought, Shelby would find irresistible. "To make this last effort," he wrote, "why not, my dear Sir, come in person? You would not object to a command that would be nominal only. I have such confidence in your wisdom that you in fact should be the guiding head and I the hand."

By then, Procter, 500 British regulars, and six guns were sailing toward Fort Meigs. Tecumseh was leading the largest Indian army ever assembled down Hull's Road. On July 21, his 3,000 Indians revealed their presence by killing seven men near the fort.

Clay, whom Harrison had left to command the 2,000 men at Fort Meigs, expected another artillery barrage. But none came. Instead, Tecumseh orchestrated on July 26 the ruse he had planned. From the woods around the road to Lower Sandusky, the Americans heard a tremendous noise. There 1,000 Indians were pretending to fight the 500 British regulars. The action, remembered Richardson, was "so animated that we were half in doubt ourselves whether the battle was a sham one or real."

The Americans, the Shawnee hoped, would think that a large relief force had been ambushed. When they opened the gates to send aid, 2,000 waiting warriors would rush into the fort. But Clay was not fooled. Finally, recalled 2d US Artillery Regiment Captain Daniel Cushing, the "heaviest thunder shower that I ever experienced" ended the charade.

Undeterred by the fiasco, Tecumseh demanded another effort. The British and Indians, he proposed, should attack Fort Stephenson. Designed by Wood, the stronghold had three blockhouses, a 16ft-high stockade, and a ditch 8ft wide and deep. There Croghan had a garrison of 167 officers and men drawn from the 17th and 24th regiments, and the Pittsburgh Blues; a 6lb gun, which his men had nicknamed "Old Betsy;" and a small quantity of ammunition.

As the reluctant British commander sailed his fleet to the mouth of the Sandusky River, 1,000 warriors followed Tecumseh to

A nephew of George Rogers Clark and William Clark, George Croghan had distinguished himself in action at Tippecanoe and Fort Meigs. This 1816 John Wesley Jarvis portrait of Croghan is at his boyhood home, Locust Grove, now a museum in Louisville. (Courtesy of Historic Locust Grove, Inc.)

Fort Stephenson. On July 30, 12 of the boldest decided to ambush 150 of Ball's dragoons a mile from the fort. At Ball's Battle, American sabers killed all but one.

On July 31, as British ships began unloading men for the assault on Croghan's fort, Shelby announced his response to the American commander's letter. On August 31, he said, the horsemen Harrison had requested would assemble at Newport, opposite Cincinnati. As a 24-year-old lieutenant, Shelby had raced to the top of a 250ft-high ridge at Point Pleasant. As a 30-year-old colonel, he had climbed 800ft to win fame on King's Mountain. Now, the 63-year-old governor weighed more that 300lb. But Harrison had known his man. "Fellow soldiers," Shelby proclaimed in his call for volunteers, "I will meet you there in person. I will lead you to the field of battle, and share with you the dangers and honors of the campaign."

On August 1, fire from five 6lb guns and a howitzer commenced the assault on Fort Stephenson. As the Americans bravely responded with occasional shots from their single gun, the bombardment continued on August 2. But it had little effect.

Tecumseh then demanded an attempt to storm the fort. Procter ordered Lieutenant-Colonel Augustus Warburton to lead 160 men against its southeastern corner, and Lieutenant-Colonel William Shortt 350 more against its northwestern. Tecumseh's Indians were to attack the southwestern corner.

TO THE
MILITIA OF KENTUCKY.

FELLOW-SOLDIERS,

YOUR government has taken measures to act effectually against the enemy in Upper Canada. Gen. Harrison, under the authority of the President of the United States, has called upon me for a strong body of troops to assist in effecting the grand objects of the campaign. The enemy in hopes to find us unprepared, has again invested Fort Meigs; but he will again be mistaken; and before you can take the field he will be driven from that post.

To comply with the requisition of Gen. Harrison, a draught might be enforced; but believing as I do, that the ardor and patriotism of my country, has not abated, and that they have waited with impatience a fair opportunity of avenging the blood of their butchered friends, I have appointed the *31st* day of *August* next, at *Newport,* for a general rendezvous of KENTUCKY VOLUNTEERS. I will meet you there in person. I will lead you to the field of battle, and share with you the dangers and honors of the campaign. Our services will not be required more than sixty days after we reach head quarters.

I invite all officers, and others possessing influence, to come forward with what mounted men they can raise: each shall command the men he may bring into the field. The superior officers will be appointed by myself at the place of general rendezvous, or on our arrival at head quarters: and I shall take pleasure in acknowledging to my country the merits and public spirit of those who may be useful in collecting a force for the present emergency.

Those who have good rifles, and know how to use them will bring them along. Those who have not, will be furnished with muskets at Newport.

Fellow Citizens! Now is the time to act; and by one decisive blow, put an end to the contest in that quarter.

ISAAC SHELBY.

Frankfort, July 31st, 1813.

Shelby's July 31, 1813 call for volunteers. (Filson Historical Society, Louisville, Kentucky)

Old Betsy today, on the lawn of the Birchard Public Library in Fremont, Ohio. (Photograph by Dale Benington)

Perry's flag survives at the US Naval Academy Museum in Annapolis, Maryland. The photograph, taken at Christmas time, shows a replica displayed in the academy's Memorial Hall. (Courtesy of the US Naval Academy)

At 5.00pm, the assault commenced. American fire halted Warburton's men far from the fort's walls. About 125 of Shortt's men reached the ditch surrounding the fort, and began hewing with axes at the walls. But Wood had anticipated such an attack. To the horror of the men at the far left of Shortt's force, a camouflaged blockhouse window opened. In it, the last thing they saw, was the barrel of Old Betsy pointed at them only 20ft away.

The blast killed Shortt and two other officers, and wounded Muir and two more. At 3.00am on August 3, the British sailed away. At a cost of 26 killed, 41 wounded, and another 29 left behind as prisoners, they had killed one American and wounded seven. "The Indians who proposed the assault, and had it not been assented to, would have forever stigmatized the British character," a bitter Procter wrote to Prévost, "scarcely came under fire before they ran off out of reach. A more than adequate sacrifice having been made to Indian opinion, I drew off the brave assailants."

Two days later, a messenger informed the American commander that a US Navy fleet was at last asail on Lake Erie. On August 19, Harrison, Cass, McArthur, Croghan, Black Hoof, and Tarhe boarded the fleet's flagship for a three-day cruise to its base at Put-in-Bay on South Bass Island. They saw waving above them on the US brig *Lawrence* a blue flag with an inscription in large, white letters. The *Lawrence*, explained the fleet's 28-year-old commander, had been named for his friend Captain James Lawrence, who had been mortally wounded in a sea engagement two months before. "Don't give up the ship," said Oliver Hazard Perry, had been his friend's last words.

FROM FORT STEPHENSON TO DETROIT

More than 3,500 horsemen responded to Shelby's call – and also a pig, which followed one of his companies from Harrodsburg. When ferries carried the Kentuckians across the Ohio, it swam the river to join them. As they rode north, the valiant pig trotted behind them, trying desperately to keep up. Every night, the Kentuckians waited for their porcine mascot around their campfires, and cheered when it finally appeared.

When the horsemen reached Urbana, Shelby visited the cabin of Simon Kenton. The old frontiersman should ride with them, Shelby told him. This was going to be something to see. At first, Kenton declined. But Shelby too had known his man. When the Kentuckians camped the following night, Kenton arrived to join them.

As Shelby's horsemen were approaching Upper Sandusky on September 12, a rowboat landed at Fort Stephenson. "We heard a tremendous shout and hurrahing," remembered Private Alfred Brunson of the 27th Infantry, "and then the booming of cannon. All eyes were turned in that direction, knowing that something glorious had occurred." Soon Harrison received a message from Perry: "We have met the enemy," the famous note began, "and they are ours."

Two days before, the *Lawrence*, its sister brig *Niagara*, and seven smaller vessels had met Barclay's *Detroit*, *Queen Charlotte* and four lesser craft. The *Lawrence*, which at first battled the whole British fleet alone, had been nearly destroyed. But Perry had transferred his flag to the *Niagara*, and then overcome the weakened *Detroit* and *Queen Charlotte*. At the September 10, 1813 battle of Lake Erie, the Americans killed 41 British sailors and marines, wounded Barclay and 92 others, captured 306 seamen and marines, and took all six British warships. The price was 27 dead and 96 wounded, almost all on the *Lawrence*.

With Shelby's Kentuckians, Harrison now had a sufficient force to move against the British by both land and water. Johnson's horsemen and four guns, he decided, would advance to Detroit on Hull's Road. Cass's, McArthur's, and Shelby's men, and the Indian warriors who had joined the Americans, would assemble at the mouth of the Portage River, and sail first to Put-in-Bay.

It would not be easy to transport thousands of men and massive quantities of supplies across Lake Erie. An illness that had arrived with Captain James Sympson's company of Donaldson's Kentucky regiment was reducing the army's numbers. But there were still too many demands for space. Many units' knapsacks and equipment, the officers concluded, would have to be transported later.

Shelby's and Ball's horses also would have to be left behind. To pen the mounts, and the Harrodsburg pig, the Kentuckians built a 2-mile-long fence across the Marblehead Peninsula. Colonel Christopher Rife and 500 Kentuckians would remain to guard them, and to cut a last road, from Lower Sandusky to the mouth of the Portage River.

At the end of the lake voyage, moreover, the Americans would conduct a joint naval and military operation that few soldiers or sailors had ever seen: an amphibious assault on an enemy beach. As Harrison's and Perry's officers planned its details, the regulars, Kentuckians, and Indians began practicing what they would do. They got so good, recalled Private Samuel Brown of Ball's dragoons, that "a company would march into a boat, debark and form on the beach in less than one minute, and that too without the least confusion."

The US brig *Niagara*, raised from the waters of Lake Erie in 1913, and now largely reconstructed, sails the lake from the Erie Maritime Museum in Erie, Pennsylvania. (Courtesy of the Flagship Niagara League; photograph by John Baker)

Two hundred and forty-one of Procter's men had been marines on Barclay's ships. Most of his guns had been on them as well. To repel an invasion, the British commander now would have only 889 regulars and 22 guns. But the most crippling consequence of Lake Erie was that no more supply boats would arrive at Amherstburg. Procter could no longer feed the Indians, nor even his own men, unless they retreated to a site where they could be supplied more easily by land.

When Procter learned of Barclay's defeat on September 12, he ordered his officers not to disclose the news to the Indians. He would tell them, he said, at a council on September 15. He then summoned Captain Matthew Dixon of the Royal Engineers and Lieutenant Felix Troughton of the Royal Artillery Regiment. They should "quietly," he said, prepare to destroy forts Detroit and Malden, and to transport the army's guns and supplies up the Thames River. Dixon and Troughton, the secretive British commander said, were not to disclose their orders to anyone. When Dixon's men began their work on September 13, Warburton complained to Procter that he had not been told. "I received for an answer," the angry colonel of the 41st remembered, "that he had a perfect right to give any secret orders that he thought proper."

On September 15, the British commander and his officers met with the Indian chiefs at a council in Amherstburg. When Procter announced that the British and Indians must fall back to a site on the Thames River, Richardson remembered, "it was evident that Tecumseh could be terrible." The Indians rose wielding their tomahawks – but there was no massacre, only an insult. Procter, the Shawnee said, was like "a fat animal that carries its tail upon its back, but when affrighted, drops it between its legs and runs off."

He would consider Tecumseh's words, the shaken British commander responded, and meet the Indians again in three days. Elliott then learned that Tecumseh planned at the September 18 council to end the British and Indian alliance with a dramatic gesture. The head of the Indian Department, Procter remembered, was "alarmed beyond measure."

As September 18 approached, the British commander asked for a meeting with Tecumseh before the council convened. On maps spread before them, Procter explained to the Shawnee that supplies now must come by wagon from Lake Ontario. The road led 5 miles to Ancaster, 15 miles further to John Norton's Mohawks at Brantford, 65 miles on to Delaware, and 30 more to Moraviantown. It then was another 25 to Chatham, a proposed village with one house on the Thames, from which large craft could carry heavy goods down the river to Lake St Clair. On the Thames, Procter said, he would build a fortified base. If the Americans pursued them, they would repel the invaders there.

The first page of Harrison's four-page order of battle for the American amphibious landing. (Filson Historical Society, Louisville, Kentucky, Mss A/B365, Beall-Booth Papers)

Where exactly, asked Tecumseh, would they fight the Americans? Harrison's army, Procter believed, would not pursue them to the Thames. But the Shawnee insisted on an answer. At Chatham, where McGregor's Creek joined the Thames, Procter hastily replied. "When I look on these 2 streams," said a satisfied Tecumseh, "I shall think of the Wabash and the Tippecanoe."

The Shawnee then met alone with the chiefs who had assembled for the council, urging them to follow the British to Chatham. Main Poc, Five Medals, and most of the others rejected his pleas. Black Hawk and his warriors left. "The British army," the Sauk later recalled, "was making preparations to retreat. I was now tired of being with them, our success being bad, and having gotten no plunder."

Tecumseh gave his speeches atop this boulder in Amherstburg, which is preserved at Fort Malden National Historic Site. (Photograph by Dale Benington)

For days, Tecumseh addressed assemblies of warriors, trying to persuade them to retreat with the British. The absence of his friend Roundhead, who had died two weeks before, hindered his effort. So did a dream by the Potawatomi chief White Pigeon, who had seen a British and Indian army defeat the Americans when they landed near Elliott's farm.

But it was too late for that. Every horse, wagon, and boat that could be found was transporting Procter's supplies toward the Thames. On September 23, the British burned Malden.

September 24 was the first anniversary of Harrison's appointment as American commander. For months in 1812, the Americans had toiled to build his network of supply roads. Now they had reaped the harvest of their

Put-in-Bay today. The towering white structure is the 325ft-high Perry's Victory and International Peace Memorial. (© John E. Rees)

François Bâby's 1812 house is now Windsor's Community Museum in Windsor, Ontario. (Author's collection)

labor. In the 12 days that followed news of Perry's victory, they had moved thousands of men and horses, and countless crates, boxes, and barrels of supplies, across Ohio to Fort Meigs and Put-in-Bay.

On September 25, the American invasion force sailed from Put-in-Bay to forward bases on Middle Sister and East Sister islands. The following day, Shane, Navarre, and Knaggs led Johnson's horsemen north from Fort Meigs toward Detroit. There a Canadian officer wrote to his parents in London: "As we are now completely in the savages' power, we are obliged in great measure to act as they think proper … I hate these savage barbarians."

At dawn on September 27, the last of the British began leaving Detroit. Warburton was leading the 41st from Sandwich to Lavalle's Farm. Johnson's horsemen were riding toward Frenchtown. On Lake Erie, Harrison's men began boarding their landing craft. It was D-Day.

Procter, Elliott, and Tecumseh were northeast of Sandwich, at the house of Colonel François Bâby, the commander of the local militia. There they waited for news from Ensign Benjamin Holmes of the Canadian Light Dragoons, who had remained south of Amherstburg to watch for the Americans' arrival. At 10.30am, Holmes reported that warships were in sight, and at 2.00pm that he could see a long line of American boats filled with soldiers.

Two hours later, the Americans were ready. Perry's officers, their guns loaded with balls attached by chains, were scanning the beach for signs of enemy defenders. Harrison's regulars, Kentuckians, and warriors were in their assigned seats, in a 1½-mile-long line of 100 boats, 25 yards apart.

Margaret Reynolds's 1813 *View of Amherstburg* shows the town as it appeared to the Americans advancing from the lower left. The Detroit River is in the center, with Bois Blanc Island to the left, Fort Malden to the right, and Amherstburg still further to the right. Elliott's Farm was to the left beyond the scene, and Girty's House beyond it. (Parks Canada Agency)

When a signal gun sounded at 4.00pm, the oarsmen began rowing the landing craft forward.

The result exceeded the Americans' highest expectations. "The landing of our army on the beach three miles south of Malden," 2d US Artillery Regiment Captain Stanton Sholes wrote in his journal, "surpassed anything of the kind ever witnessed. All of our boats landed at one and the same time. In less than 2 minutes after the first boat struck the shore, no less than 4,000 troops and 6 pieces of artillery all landed, completely formed in a line of battle."

The Americans, who found on the beach no enemy to fight, were within minutes marching toward Amherstburg. Concerned at what the Kentuckians might do there, Harrison had directed their captains to read to them a special order. "Remember the River Raisin," it said, "but remember it only whilst victory is suspended. The revenge of a soldier cannot be gratified on a fallen enemy."

The warning was apt. "About a half mile below Malden," wrote Sholes, "is the dwelling house of our savage enemy Col. Elliott … A small distance from Elliott's is the deserted dwelling of that well-known Simon Girty." But the only revenge taken was a ransacking of Elliott's house. Kenton, who had raced ahead to Girty's with Simrall's advance guard, saw that his old friend reached safety among John Norton's Mohawks.

On the following day, as a heavy rain began to fall, Harrison's army advanced toward Sandwich. The 41st marched from Lavalle's to the River Ruscom. Procter, Elliott, and Tecumseh remained at Bâby's.

On September 29, as the 41st trod in a downpour on to Trudelle's Farm, Procter rode to join them. Elliott, Tecumseh, and the Indians who had chosen to follow the Shawnee retreated to the River Ruscom. About 2.00pm the Americans reached Detroit. "Just before we landed," Brown remembered, "the inhabitants hoisted the U. S. flag amid the acclamations of thousands."

FROM DETROIT TO MORAVIANTOWN

On September 30, Elliott, Tecumseh, and 5,000 Indians marched 15 miles from the River Ruscom to join Procter and the 41st at Trudelle's. The Shawnee had persuaded about a third of the Indians to follow him, 1,200 warriors and their families. Beyond Trudelle's, the large transports *Miamis*, *Mary*, and *Ellen*, the *General Myers* and *Eliza*, and several smaller boats were carrying the British Army's heavy supplies up the Thames toward Chatham. At Dolsen's Landing, where the British had established a commissary, ovens were baking bread.

A dreary parade of Canadian refugees and wagons had begun to reach the ferry that crossed the Thames to Dolsen's. From his nearby farmhouse, Thomas McCrae saw them. "This morning," he wrote in his journal, "still raining and rained all day. The roads are most shocking bad. The people from Malden are all flocking up on their way, the Americans having taken possession of Malden on Monday last."

Harrison, who was in Sandwich, had recovered Detroit and taken Malden. But his greater hope, to end the British–Indian alliance, remained unfulfilled. To accomplish that, he thought, there must be a battle like Fallen Timbers.

The Americans, however, could not pursue their retreating enemies. Most of their equipment was still in Ohio. His whole army, Harrison wrote to Meigs, had only one horse, a "miserable French pony" that had been found for Shelby to ride. At noon, however, Johnson's horsemen reached Detroit. An elated Harrison ordered them to cross the river to Sandwich immediately.

Early on October 1, the American commander met with his senior officers. As much of the army as possible, he ordered, would pursue Procter immediately. A hasty investigation revealed that Johnson's horsemen, Shelby's dismounted Kentuckians, four companies of Cass's brigade, and the Americans' Indian allies would be ready to march the next morning with two guns, enough ammunition, and several days of beef rations. Three warships and 50 boats would carry its heavy equipment and supplies as far up the Thames as possible. The rest of Cass's brigade would follow as soon as its equipment arrived from Ohio. McArthur's brigade and 100 of the Indians would remain to guard Detroit and the Canadian territory the Americans had occupied.

For operations in the Thames area, the Americans would have an excellent guide. Matthew Dolsen, whose son John had the ferry and landing, had fled from Uppermost Canada after Hull's retreat. A 25-mile march from Sandwich, he said, would take the army to the River Ruscom. By a 19-mile march on October 3 it then could reach a good campsite on the Thames. There, at John Drake's Farm, the army could rendezvous with its supply flotilla.

As Harrison's and Perry's officers worked feverishly to prepare for the next morning's advance, Procter was traveling toward Moraviantown. Warburton, who knew nothing of Procter's plans, or his promise to Tecumseh, received a report that American ships had been seen at the mouth of the Thames. The alarmed commander of the 41st then sent a messenger to ask Procter to return to Trudelle's.

An annoyed Procter rode back. When he reached Dolsen's Landing in late afternoon, he found the 41st Regiment crossing the river, and Tecumseh and the Indians camping on the south bank at McCrae's Farm. He had fallen back from Trudelle's, Warburton said, to ensure that the Americans would not overtake the retreating army.

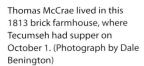

Thomas McCrae lived in this 1813 brick farmhouse, where Tecumseh had supper on October 1. (Photograph by Dale Benington)

At dawn on October 2, Procter rode to the mouth of the Thames, where he saw what he had expected: no American ships. When he returned, the annoyed British commander summoned several of his officers for a conference. To display his displeasure at his unnecessary recall, he did not invite to the meeting Warburton and his principal subordinates, Evans and Muir. He instead met with Elliott, Troughton, Dixon, and Captain William Crowther of the 41st. Dixon, who had examined Dolsen's Landing and Chatham, reviewed their defects as locations for Procter's fortified base. Moraviantown, he thought, might be better.

The Thames River to Moraviantown.

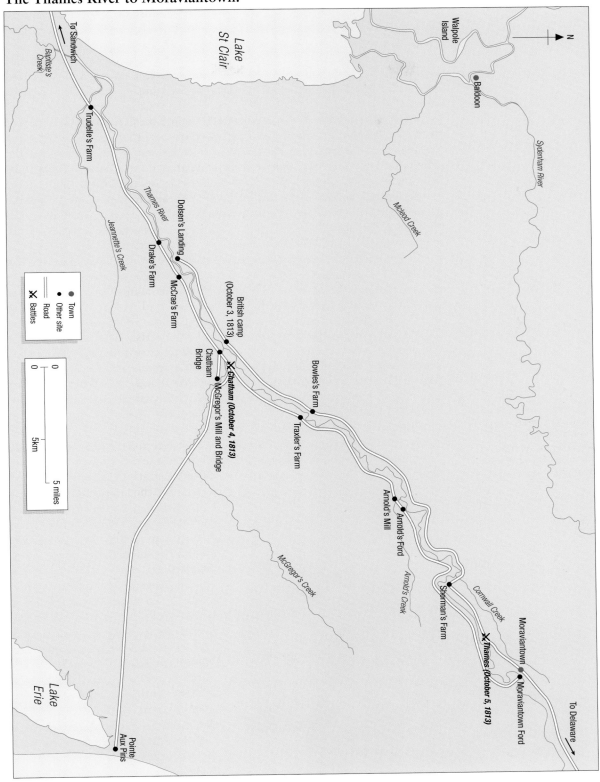

To Sandwich

Baptiste's Creek

Lake St Clair

Walpole Island

Baldoon

Sydenham River

N

Trudelle's Farm

Jeanette's Creek

Thames River

Mcleod Creek

Dolsen's Landing

Drake's Farm

McCrae's Farm

British camp
(October 3, 1813)

Chatham Bridge

McGregor's Mill and Bridge

✗ Chatham (October 4, 1813)

Bowles's Farm

Traxler's Farm

Arnold's Mill

Arnold's Ford

Arnold's Creek

Sherman's Farm

Cornwall Creek

McGregor's Creek

Moraviantown

✗ Thames (October 5, 1813)

Moraviantown Ford

To Delaware

Lake Erie

Pointe Aux Pins

Legend
- ● Town
- ● Other site
- ═ Road
- ✗ Battles

0   5km
0   5 miles

By then, the Americans were advancing from Sandwich. "The army," remembered Shelby, "was on its march by sunrise on the morning of the 2d of October." The still-spreading sickness, and discontent at the prospect of fighting on foot, had reduced the numbers he led. The Kentuckians left behind, remembered a scoffing Private William Greathouse of Renick's regiment, "something like 1,000 men that professed to be sick. But I told them that I was determined to go so long as I could lift one leg past the other."

Riding with Johnson's horsemen, Harrison led the way. Cass, who was with him, had left Owings to lead his brigade forward. Perry, who had asked to accompany Harrison as his aide, was with the American commander too. He had left to lead the supply flotilla his second-in-command, Matthew Elliott's American nephew Master Commandant Jesse Elliott.

Behind the horsemen, Shelby led his 10 Kentucky regiments and Paull the four companies of regulars, three from his 27th Regiment and one from Owings's 24th. Wood commanded the army's two 6lb guns. Black Hoof, Tarhe, and John and William Conner led the 150 Indians.

By the end of the day, the Americans had reached the River Ruscom. The next day, Dolsen said, they would cross bridges over Baptiste's and Jeannette's creeks, and pass Louis Trudelle's Farm. Then they would reach the Thames and camp at John Drake's Farm.

At the first light on October 3, the British commander sent Holmes and 17 dragoons to destroy the Jeannette's Creek bridge. Procter then left for Moraviantown with Dixon and Crowther. At Chatham, they found that the army's two great 24lb guns already had been unloaded. Before resuming his journey with Dixon, Procter ordered Crowther to prepare to fortify the site. The British captain then began a search for the army's entrenching tools. They had been packed, he soon learned, beneath tons of ammunition and other supplies on the *Mary* and *Ellen*.

By then, Johnson's men had reached Jeannette's Creek, where they captured Holmes and his dragoons. About two hours after Procter's departure from Dolsen's, the riderless mount of one of the Canadian horsemen reached the British camp. After sending a messenger to inform Procter, Warburton sent another to Crowther. The British supply flotilla, he ordered, must retire further up the river, to Bowles's Farm.

The alarmed commander of the 41st then prepared for battle. He formed his units on the north side of the Thames, and asked Tecumseh to position his warriors to fight at McCrae's. The Indians, the Shawnee responded, would move back to Chatham. "That," his message told a puzzled Warburton, "was the place where a stand was promised to be made."

This lithograph from Benson Lossing's *Pictorial Field-Book of the War of 1812* shows the appearance of John Dolsen's cabin at Dolsen's Landing in 1860. (Author's collection)

Warburton then led the 41st up the river toward Bowles's. When the British reached the ground opposite the mouth of McGregor's Creek, they heard loud noises across the Thames at Chatham. Tecumseh, Richardson remembered, was addressing the Indians in a "loud and violent manner." The Shawnee, who had expected to see at Chatham a fortified position bristling with artillery, had instead found only the two unloaded guns, and abandoned piles of unpacked ammunition and supplies.

Elliott, who crossed the river to investigate, returned in terror. Warburton, who was baffled at the Indians' rage, asked the head of the Indian Department to calm them while the army resumed its retreat to Bowles's. "I will not, by God," Elliott replied, "stay and be sacrificed."

Then a messenger from Tecumseh arrived. The Shawnee, Bullock remembered, said that "we should not proceed beyond the ground we then occupied, that Gen. Procter had promised them to await the enemy on that ground and fight them, and had also promised to erect fortifications there." Warburton, Richardson recalled, "did not appear to know how to act, the general not having left any directions, but he decided on falling in with the wishes of the Indians." But when Tecumseh asked Warburton to cross the Thames to join his warriors, the suspicious British colonel refused. The 41st then camped opposite the mouth of McGregor's Creek, expecting to be attacked at any minute by the Americans, or perhaps the Indians.

Warburton sent Captain Thomas Coleman of the Canadian Light Dragoons to tell Procter that he must return at once. The Canadian captain left behind a corps of 41st Regiment officers on the verge of mutiny. Lieutenant Benjamin Geale told Richardson "that a council of war was going to assemble immediately in order to decide whether or not the command should be taken from the general." But Warburton was unwilling to accept it. Muir, Richardson remembered, said that Procter "ought to be hanged for being away, and that Col. Warburton ought to be hanged for not assuming the command."

An hour before dark, Procter and Dixon arrived at Moraviantown. After inspecting the site, the British commander concluded that it would be a better base than Chatham. Dixon, he ordered, should the next day begin fortifying the high ground near the village.

The roads along the Thames took crooked courses, moving from bend to bend of the river. Philip John Bainbridge's *Bush Farm Near Chatham* shows the appearance in 1838 of the road on which Warburton retreated from Dolsen's. (Library and Archives Canada/Philip John Bainbridge collection/c011811)

Shortly after he retired, Warburton's first messenger awoke Procter. The annoyed British commander returned to bed. A few hours later, Coleman arrived. Procter sent the dragoon captain back with a message. He would meet Warburton and the 41st at Bowles's the next morning.

The Americans ended the day at Drake's Farm, where they met Jesse Elliott's supply flotilla. The British, Harrison knew from the captured dragoons, had crossed the Thames, and camped the night before at Dolsen's Landing, 4 miles ahead. From there, Dolsen said, roads led 29 miles to Moraviantown on both sides of the river. The north bank road then went on from Moraviantown to Delaware.

To pursue their enemies, the Americans must cross the river either by watercraft or at a ford. The river, Dolsen said, would remain navigable by Jesse Elliott's warships for another 14 miles upstream, to Peter Traxler's Farm on the south bank, and Bowles's on the north. It would be dangerous, Perry advised, for the American watercraft to go any further up the narrowing Thames.

The first ford, said Harrison's guide, was 22 miles ahead on the south bank road, about a mile beyond Theophilus Arnold's Mill. The next was 12 miles further, where the road ended across from Moraviantown. But 8 miles ahead, Dolsen cautioned, the road would reach Chatham, where McGregor's Creek was too deep to ford. Two bridges crossed it. The road used the Chatham bridge, at the mouth of the creek. But from there, another road led up McGregor's Creek to Point Aux Pins on Lake Erie. A mile up that road, at John McGregor's Mill, there was another bridge across the creek.

The Americans, Harrison decided, would not cross the Thames yet. Elliott's flotilla would remain at Drake's, guarded by two companies of the 27th. The army would advance further on the south bank, and cross the Thames at Arnold's or the Moraviantown Ford.

Early on October 4, Warburton marched 6 miles to Bowles's Farm, where he found Procter, Crowther, the British boats, and piles of unloaded ammunition and supplies everywhere. He left behind at Chatham Tecumseh and his angry chiefs. There soon would be no food for the women and children, the Shawnee told his followers. They must move east toward Moraviantown, where the British could feed them. The warriors should remain at Chatham, and delay the Americans while the women and children retreated.

Many of the Indians had had enough. Hundreds began moving through the woods back toward Sandwich. But Tecumseh, with the aid of the Ottawa chief Naiwash, persuaded the rest. As about 2,400 Indian women and children

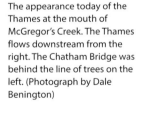

The appearance today of the Thames at the mouth of McGregor's Creek. The Thames flows downstream from the right. The Chatham Bridge was behind the line of trees on the left. (Photograph by Dale Benington)

began moving along the road to Arnold's Mill, the Shawnee sent a message to Procter. Tecumseh's warriors, the relieved British commander learned, would delay the Americans at Chatham and join the British in Moraviantown.

Warburton, Procter ordered, should lead the 41st there, where Troughton was to assemble all the artillery he could find. The British commander remained at Bowles's with Crowther, 144 soldiers, and the crews of the British boats. As they worked feverishly, trying to unload needed supplies and find ways to transport them from Bowles's to Moraviantown, 800 warriors were destroying the McGregor's Creek bridges and assuming battle positions.

By then, Johnson's horsemen were nearing Chatham. Just before they reached McGregor's Creek, McAfee remembered, "a woman who appeared to have been sent as our guardian angel came to us in the wood." Hundreds of Indians, she warned, were waiting ahead for the Americans.

Harrison ordered his army to form and advance in line of battle. "We marched on the extreme right of the foot troops," recalled McAfee, "over the worst logs, swamps and brush I ever saw. About twelve o'clock the firing commenced on our left and our cannon opened at the bridge at the mouth of creek." The American guns quickly drove the Indians from the Chatham bridge, which had been imperfectly destroyed. There was heavier fighting on the right when Johnson's horsemen reached the McGregor's Mill bridge. "But half an hour," McAfee remembered, "put us in possession of the bridge and whole Indian camp." The American casualties, Harrison reported, were two killed and four wounded.

When Procter learned that the Americans were at Chatham, he left Bowles's Farm for Moraviantown. The unloaded ammunition and supplies, he ordered, were to be burned. The *Miamis*, *Mary*, and *Ellen*, which could go no further upstream, were to be scuttled to block the advance of the American flotilla. The *Eliza*, *General Myers*, and smaller watercraft were to go as far up the Thames as possible. Crowther was to unload their cargos and see that they were transported to Moraviantown.

By 2.00pm, the Americans had repaired the bridges and were advancing again. After a march of 5 miles, they reached Traxler's Farm. "The British or Indians," McAfee wrote in his journal, "had set fire to a fine schooner with two masts loaded with muskets, cannon-balls and military stores of an immense amount." Across the river, they could see the ammunition unloaded at Bowles's afire. "Every eight or ten minutes," McAfee remembered, a bomb would burst."

One of the scuttled British vessels, probably the *Miamis*, was raised in 1903 with 2 tons of surviving munitions. The photograph shows it in Chatham's Tecumseh Park. (Chatham-Kent Museum, 952.10.1)

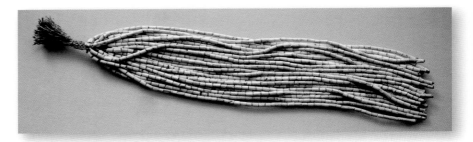

Wampum comprised quarter-inch-long bored beads made from clam and whelk shells. The Indians, who used them as currency, also threaded them into belts to record important events. Tecumseh gave Matthew Elliott these strings of wampum as a present in 1813. (Parks Canada Agency)

After watching the fireworks display, the Americans remained at Traxler's, where their cautious commander ordered breastworks built. The 41st halted at Sherman's Farm, 4 miles short of Moraviantown. Tecumseh and the Indians camped at Arnold's Mill.

Moraviantown, Dolsen advised, was 21 miles ahead. If the British remained there, Harrison concluded, the Americans could overtake them the next day. A messenger, however, then arrived from Owings, who was advancing rapidly with Cass's brigade. If the American commander waited at Traxler's for two days, he would have another 700 regulars.

About 7.00pm, Harrison announced his decision. "After dark," McAfee wrote in his journal, "Col. Johnson collected us together. Gen. Harrison soon came up and directed us to furnish ourselves with beef for a forced march tomorrow. He was determined if possible to bring them to a stand."

The American commander, McAfee remembered, then was busy "till 10 o'clock, superintending and inspecting all the arrangements of the camp." Shelby was up almost all night, "going round every part of his lines to see that proper vigilance was preserved, till exhausted with fatigue he took up his lodging in that part of the camp nearest the enemy, where he shared the blanket of one of his soldiers."

Before he retired, Brigadier-General Joseph Desha, who commanded four of Shelby's regiments, received a visit from an old friend. In 1775, William Whitley, his wife, and their two children had been among the first Kentucky settlers. In 1787, he had built the first brick house in Kentucky, with walls four bricks thick, and secret rooms and passages to escape Indian raiders. In 17 battles against the Indians, he had taken 12 scalps.

When Johnson had called for horsemen, the 64-year-old frontiersman had

Whitley's house is now the William Whitley House State Historic Site, near Stanford, Kentucky. (Graphic Enterprises/ *Pioneer Times*)

volunteered to ride with Captain James Davidson's company. "In vain," Davidson remembered, "his friends attempted to deter him." Atop his magnificent horse Emperor, Whitley had soon become an instantly recognizable figure in Harrison's army. On his head was a tricorn hat he had worn since the Revolutionary War. Across his chest, to hold his powder horn and bag of balls, there was not the usual leather strap, but a wide belt of white Indian wampum.

He was forming, Whitley told Desha, a band of horsemen to go ahead of the rest in the coming battle. They would be a Forlorn Hope, attracting fire that otherwise would endanger those charging behind them. And tomorrow, he told his friend, was going to be his last day.

THE BATTLE OF THE THAMES

October 5: 6.00am–12.00pm

When the sun appeared at 6.29am, Harrison's army was marching toward Arnold's Mill. Ahead, the Indian commanders John and William Conner knew, lay a town of Christian Delawares like those they had lived in as boys. In 1792, David Zeisberger had left their Michigan Territory village to found it. He had named it Schönfeld – Fairfield in English – but everyone called it Moraviantown.

The Moravians, Protestants from what would become the Czech Republic, had sent Zeisberger to North America to convert the Ohio Indians. In 1772, he had begun founding Ohio villages like Schönbrunn and Gnadenhütten. But during the Revolutionary War, the British had thought that the Christian Delaware were aiding the Americans. In 1781, Elliott had herded them to Captives' Town, a concentration camp near Upper Sandusky where many had starved. The Americans had thought they were enemy Indians. In 1782, Pennsylvania militiamen had killed 96 of the Captives' Town survivors at Gnadenhütten. Later The Prophet had concluded that they were witches; in 1806, his followers had begun burning them.

For decades, the Christian Delaware had searched for a haven from war and persecution. They had not found it on the Thames. On October 3, Procter had appropriated Moraviantown for use as a British base. Now he was there with 250 men, and the expelled Christian Delawares at a refugee camp 6 miles up the river.

On high ground near Moraviantown, the British commander had decided, he would await the Americans. His men would fight on the left, and the Indians on the right. When Warburton's soldiers arrived from Sherman's Farm and Crowther's with the supplies, he would have 800 men. Troughton would have 16 guns, and ammunition for them when Crowther returned.

When Procter still had not heard from Crowther at 8.00am, he sent his dragoons to hasten transport of the supplies. But Johnson's horsemen reached them first. "By nine o'clock," recalled Harrison, "we were at Arnold's mill, having taken, in the course of the morning, two gun boats, and several batteaux, loaded with provisions and ammunition."

By then, Tecumseh's warriors had crossed the Thames at the Moraviantown Ford, and begun searching in the woods upstream for campsites where their women and children would be safe. Then they began arriving in Moraviantown.

At 10.00am, Procter learned that Crowther had been captured, and most of the supplies lost. His frustration grew when he showed arriving Indian

Moraviantown had a church, a schoolhouse, and about 50 log cabins. This photograph of Schoenbrunn Village, a reconstructed Moravian town near New Philadelphia, Ohio, gives an impression of its general appearance. (Author's photograph)

chiefs the field on which they would fight. The ground he had assigned to them, they protested, provided no cover. The trees there, scoffed Captain William Caldwell of the Indian Department, were "all scrubby bushes."

Tecumseh, who had been the last to leave Arnold's Mill, finally arrived and inspected the field. They would fight, the Shawnee announced, at a better site 2 miles downstream. There, about 40 yards from the river, the road from Sherman's Farm passed through a dense forest of large beech, maple, and walnut trees with little underbrush. The woods covered the ground from the river to the edge of a small swamp, about 250 yards beyond the road, which extended toward Sherman's on a course roughly paralleling the road. The small swamp, 50–75 yards wide and 700 yards long, was a treacherous morass of mud, deep pools, and rotting vegetation, impassable by horses. Beyond the small swamp was a much larger mire, known as Backmetack Marsh. Between the two swamps, an isthmus of high ground extended toward Sherman's Farm for the length of the small swamp, widening as it went from 100 to 450 yards. There the ground was thickly treed, but, unlike that between the river and the small swamp, full of thickets and undergrowth.

After inspecting the site with Tecumseh, and agreeing that it would be the battlefield, Procter rode back to Moraviantown. By then, the Americans had begun crossing the 3ft-deep Thames at the ford beyond Arnold's Mill. "Each horseman," remembered McAfee, "was ordered by Gen. Harrison to take one of the foot behind him and cross the river in that order, Col. Trotter's regiment advanced and we each carried one man over."

Like every boy in Uppermost Canada, 10-year-old David Sherman had hoped to see among the retreating British and Indians the now legendary Tecumseh. In Moraviantown, he thought, he might get a glimpse. After walking 2 miles from his father's farm toward the town, he found an Indian in a buckskin shirt and leggings sitting on a log.

His face was painted black and red. From his nose hung a ring, and from his neck a silver medallion. An ostrich feather, Sherman remembered 50 years later, rose from a turban wrapped around his head. Tecumseh, who could speak English when he wanted to, asked the boy his name and where he lived. When Sherman told him, the Shawnee said, "Go back and stay home, for there will be a fight here soon."

12.00pm–2.30pm

By noon, the Americans were moving forward from the ford. Whitley, however, stayed behind on the north bank of the Thames. The frontiersman, Davidson remembered, had "caught sight of four Indians on the opposite side and lingered behind, trying to get a shot at them. We went on, and when we had gotten about a mile on our road, we were overtaken by Whitley, who rode up with a triumphant air, holding aloft the scalp of an Indian." Now, he told Captain Young Ewing of Barbour's regiment, he had 13.

Whitley claimed his 13th scalp with this rifle. (Photograph by Kenneth Orr)

Twenty men had enlisted in Whitley's band of bold riders. Brigadier-General Samuel Caldwell's 25-year-old aide Charles Wickliffe was eager to join them. "After crossing the Thames," Wickliffe remembered, "I obtained the consent of General Samuel Caldwell to attach myself to Whitley's Forlorn Hope." But the quality of Wickliffe's steed did not match his daring. "Upon trying, I found my Canadian pony unable to keep pace with the Kentucky horses upon which Whitley and his men were mounted, and had to fall back to my brigade."

Charles Wickliffe would later serve as Kentucky governor, and would play an important role in securing the state for the Union during the Civil War. Wickland, Wickliffe's 1825 house in Bardstown, Kentucky, is now a museum. (Graphic Enterprises/*Pioneer Times*)

At the head of an American column about 2½ miles long, Johnson's horsemen rode cautiously. They advanced, McAfee remembered, "expecting battle every moment." But their pace was still hard for men on foot to follow. "We marched a forced march all the time in a good dog trot," remembered Greathouse.

About 1.30pm, Warburton's 475 men reached the battlefield with a 6lb gun. At 2.00pm, Procter arrived with 45 dragoons. He had left Troughton, 130 men, and 15 guns on the high ground at Moraviantown, to which the British would retreat if forced to fall back, and at the village 70 men too ill to fight. The British commander, recalled Bullock, ordered the 41st to "form up across the road … The formation was made in the greatest confusion."

By then, Johnson's men were beyond Sherman's Farm. Soon they overtook a wagon filled with ammunition. The British Army, the luckless driver said, was only a few hundred yards ahead. A messenger sped back to Sherman's Farm to inform the American commander.

At 2.15pm, remembered McAfee, "General Harrison came riding up and sent Maj. Wood, the commander of the artillery with a spy-glass to view the situation of the enemy." Harrison then ordered the American units to advance and form their battle lines. The deployment, Brigadier-General Joseph Desha estimated, would take about an hour and a half.

2.30pm–3.15pm

By 2.30pm, American units were marching from Sherman's Farm to the site where they would form for battle. A half-mile beyond the site, Procter was waiting with 550 British and Canadians and one gun, and Tecumseh with 800 warriors.

Three hundred yards ahead of Procter and his guard of 35 dragoons, Lieutenant William Gardiner's 6lb gun crew had a clear line of sight for 300 yards down the road. On Gardiner's left were Cornet Pierre Lefevre and 10 dragoons. Ten yards to his right, a two-rank line of 41st regulars began to extend to the small swamp. Where their line was not interrupted by trees, Warburton's 475 infantrymen stood in close order, shoulder to shoulder.

To the right of the British were the Indians. For hours, they had searched for safe paths through the swamps and dragged timbers to create breastworks at their positions. Now they were in an almost half-mile-long line curving forward through Backmetack Marsh. Elliott was at their center. His Indian

At Fallen Timbers, Colonel William Caldwell had led two companies of Canadian militiamen dressed as Indians to conceal their origin. His small company of Caldwell's Rangers fought at Thames in the uniform worn by these re-enactors. (Parks Canada Agency – Brenna Houston)

This 1858 daguerreotype depicts the Ojibwe chief Oshawana, also known as John Naudee. (Library and Archives Canada, /e010797042)

Department subordinates were on the flanks of the three main Indian units, their left wing, center, and right wing.

About 270 warriors were in the Indian left wing, which contained Creek, Delaware, and Shawnee warriors who followed Tecumseh; Potawatomis of Shabbona's and Mad Sturgeon's bands; and Wyandots led by Roundhead's brother, Split Log. With them were Colonel William Caldwell's 25 Canadian frontiersmen. Caldwell's son Captain William Caldwell was at the wing's far left. Tecumseh, the wing's commander, was at its far right. With him were his friends Shabbona and Mad Sturgeon, and two men from the British Indian Department. One was another Caldwell son, the Potawatomi Billy Caldwell. The other was the adopted Shawnee Andrew Clark, who served as Tecumseh's interpreter.

About 260 Ottawas and Ojibwes were in the Indian center. There Naiwash led the Ottawas and Winepagon his band of Ojibwes. Another 260 Ojibwes, Winnebagos, Fox, Kickapoos, and Sauks were in the right wing. There Oshawana and Peckickee led their Ojibwe followers, and Four Legs and Naw Kaw their bands of Winnebagos.

When the Indians were in their battle positions, Tecumseh met with Procter to coordinate the British and Indian movements. The first shot from the 6lb gun, they agreed, was to be the signal for the Indians to attack the Americans' left flank. Tecumseh then told the British commander, Procter's aide Captain John Hall remembered, "that our men were too thickly posted, that they would be exposed to the enemy's riflemen, and thrown away to no advantage."

The British commander ordered the 41st to reform. Gardiner's gun and artillerymen, and

Lefevre's dragoons would remain in the same position. Warburton's men, however, were to extend their position to occupy ground between the small swamp and Backmetack Marsh. They were to form in two lines, in open order, about 3ft apart.

Procter's original line of 475 men became a line of only 240, led by Evans. The 155 men in Bullock's and another company, led by Muir, formed a second line, which extended from 200 yards behind Evans's left to 100 behind his right. Lieutenant Harris Hailes's light company, which moved beyond the small swamp, formed in two 50-yard long lines of 40 men.

Tecumseh then inspected the reformed British formations. "The haughty chieftain," Richardson remembered, passed along our line, pleased with the manner in which his left was supported, and seemingly sanguine of success." He "pressed the hand of each officer," the young ensign recalled, "and then passed away forever from our view."

His disciplined regulars, the British commander thought, would easily repel Harrison's horde of unruly American militiamen. He "awaited the results of the attack," Procter recalled, "with full confidence." But some of his officers did not share his aplomb. The British lines, thought a worried Bullock, were in "a remarkably thick forest." "It was impossible," remembered Richardson, "for the view to extend itself beyond a distance of twenty paces."

3.15pm–4.00pm

The numbers in the American units had dwindled further during their pursuit of the British and Indians. "The whole way from Sandwich to the battleground," recalled McAfee, "was filled with scattering parties of the militia." Of the 69 men who had crossed the Ohio in Sympson's company, only 37 now would take their places in the American ranks.

For the coming battle, Harrison would have 1,760 of Shelby's dismounted Kentuckians, 130 US Army infantrymen and artillerymen, 150 Indians, and 960 of Johnson's horsemen. Shelby's men, the regulars and the Indians, he planned, would battle the British on the right. Johnson's horsemen would attack Tecumseh's Indians on the left.

On the left, an unhappy Johnson told his commander, his men would be unable to use their horses to advantage. The woods there rose from a maze of thickets and dense undergrowth. Beyond, in Backmetack Marsh, the ground was worse. But on the right, Johnson said, there was little undergrowth and no swamp. There his horsemen could charge through the woods, and attack the British line.

As Harrison considered Johnson's idea, Wood returned after yet another look at the British with his telescope. Procter, he reported, had redeployed. The men in his line now were in open order.

Johnson's proposal alarmed the Corps of Engineers captain. Trained cavalrymen and dragoons, Wood knew, charged infantry lines

Richard M. Johnson, who survived five wounds at the battle, inherited at his father's death in 1815 the slave Julia Chinn. As unafraid of social conventions as he was of Indians, he announced that she was now Mrs Richard Johnson. This 1895 bust of Johnson by James Paxton Voorhees is in the US Senate Chamber. (Author's collection)

The British artillerymen and dragoons could see nothing on the empty road, and the men of the 41st nothing beyond the furthest visible trees, about 30 yards ahead. But the alarmed British soldiers began to hear what sounded like distant thunder. Then the ground began to tremble, and the sound and shaking grew ever greater.

Thirty seconds after beginning to trot, the lead riders reached Suggett's cheering men, who began moving forward after them. After another 30 seconds, they sped up into a gallop. Racing at more than 20 miles an hour; the men at the head of the files were avoiding branches, trunks and fallen logs nearly every second. After another 15 seconds, the sight they were looking for appeared. Behind the trees ahead there were redcoats.

When the horsemen at the head of Johnson's columns burst from behind their cover, they were moving at a speed that would take them into Evans's line in three seconds. The shocked British officers shouted, "Fire!" Balls came, McAfee remembered, "at the distance of twenty steps" from the British line. But they were too late, too few, and too badly aimed to do much damage.

The four columns of horsemen exploded through the stunned British. "I do not think," recalled Warburton, "a man of the first line loaded a second time. They immediately dispersed, some towards the second line, some into the wood. The officers were calling in all directions, but it had no effect."

The men in the second line, Bullock recalled, heard "a heavy firing of musketry" ahead. When the Kentuckians appeared, Muir's men "fired an irregular volley obliquing to the right and left." But the horsemen, Bullock remembered, "advanced so close before the reserve could commence firing, from the number of trees, that before a third round could be fired they broke through the left."

"After giving us a fire," McAfee recalled, Muir's line "was also broken and thrown into confusion. Our columns, having passed through, wheeled to the right and left, and began to pour a destructive fire on the rear of their disordered ranks. In a moment the contest was over. No sooner had our horsemen charged through their lines and gained their rear, than they began to surrender as fast as they could throw down their arms."

When Procter heard the fire, he rode forward on the road to investigate. He first passed Lefevre's fleeing dragoons and runaway horses pulling the 6lb gun's carriage. "The gun," he later complained, "was in the possession of the enemy immediately as the attack commenced, without having fired a shot." "The unfortunate six-pounder," remembered Harrison's aide David Trimble, "was found loaded, primed and ready to fire with 40–50 rounds of fixed ammunition lying by her."

The British commander then saw ahead sprinting redcoats without muskets, and American horsemen behind them. He and his dragoon escort turned and fled toward Delaware. When they reached Moraviantown, Troughton asked what he was to do with his guns. Procter's reply, the bewildered artillery commander remembered, was: "Do the best you could, or to that effect."

In three minutes, James Johnson's horsemen had destroyed the British Army. The 80 men in the light company, isolated beyond the small swamp, alone remained. The cost, moreover, had been negligible. Captain John Berry and two others had been wounded. "It is," observed an astonished Wood, "really a novel thing that raw militia stuck upon horses, with muskets in their hands instead of sabers, should be able to pierce British lines with such effect. Perhaps the only circumstance which could justify that deviation from the long established rules of the art military is the complete success of the result."

Private Robert Collins of Combs's company blew on this hunting horn the signal for Colonel Richard Johnson's horsemen to advance. (Kentucky Historical Society, 1904.23)

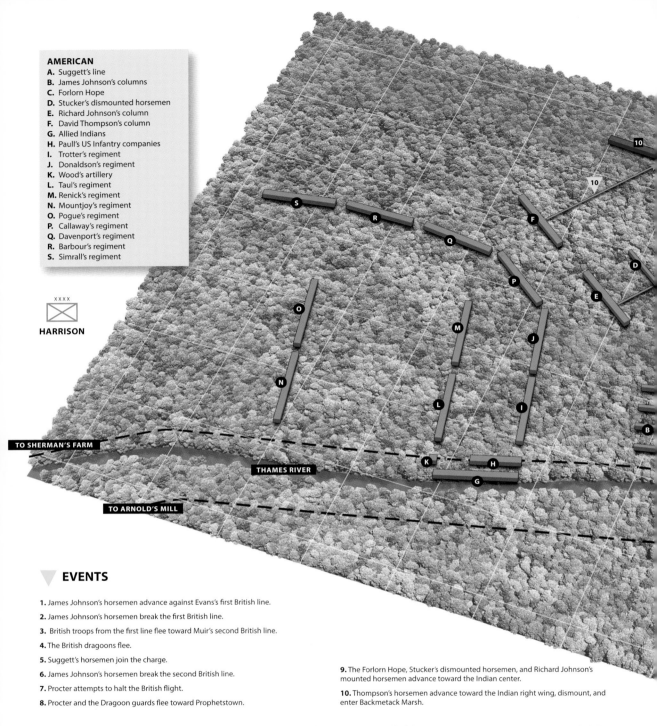

AMERICAN
A. Suggett's line
B. James Johnson's columns
C. Forlorn Hope
D. Stucker's dismounted horsemen
E. Richard Johnson's column
F. David Thompson's column
G. Allied Indians
H. Paull's US Infantry companies
I. Trotter's regiment
J. Donaldson's regiment
K. Wood's artillery
L. Taul's regiment
M. Renick's regiment
N. Mountjoy's regiment
O. Pogue's regiment
P. Callaway's regiment
Q. Davenport's regiment
R. Barbour's regiment
S. Simrall's regiment

xxxx
HARRISON

TO SHERMAN'S FARM

THAMES RIVER

TO ARNOLD'S MILL

EVENTS

1. James Johnson's horsemen advance against Evans's first British line.

2. James Johnson's horsemen break the first British line.

3. British troops from the first line flee toward Muir's second British line.

4. The British dragoons flee.

5. Suggett's horsemen join the charge.

6. James Johnson's horsemen break the second British line.

7. Procter attempts to halt the British flight.

8. Procter and the Dragoon guards flee toward Prophetstown.

9. The Forlorn Hope, Stucker's dismounted horsemen, and Richard Johnson's mounted horsemen advance toward the Indian center.

10. Thompson's horsemen advance toward the Indian right wing, dismount, and enter Backmetack Marsh.

THE AMERICAN ATTACK, OCTOBER 5, 4.00PM–4.20PM

After a four-day pursuit of Major-General Henry Procter's British soldiers and Tecumseh's Indian warriors, Brigadier-General William Henry Harrison's Kentucky militiamen found them waiting for battle on October 5, 1813 on a wooded field a mile and a half east of present Thamesville, Ontario. The engagement began at 4.00pm with an unexpected, and unprecedented, maneuver. Lieutenant-Colonel James Johnson led 480 Kentucky mounted riflemen in a galloping charge through thick woods against 400 regular British infantrymen deployed in two lines at the far left of the British and Indian position.

Note: Gridlines are shown at intervals of 150m (492ft)

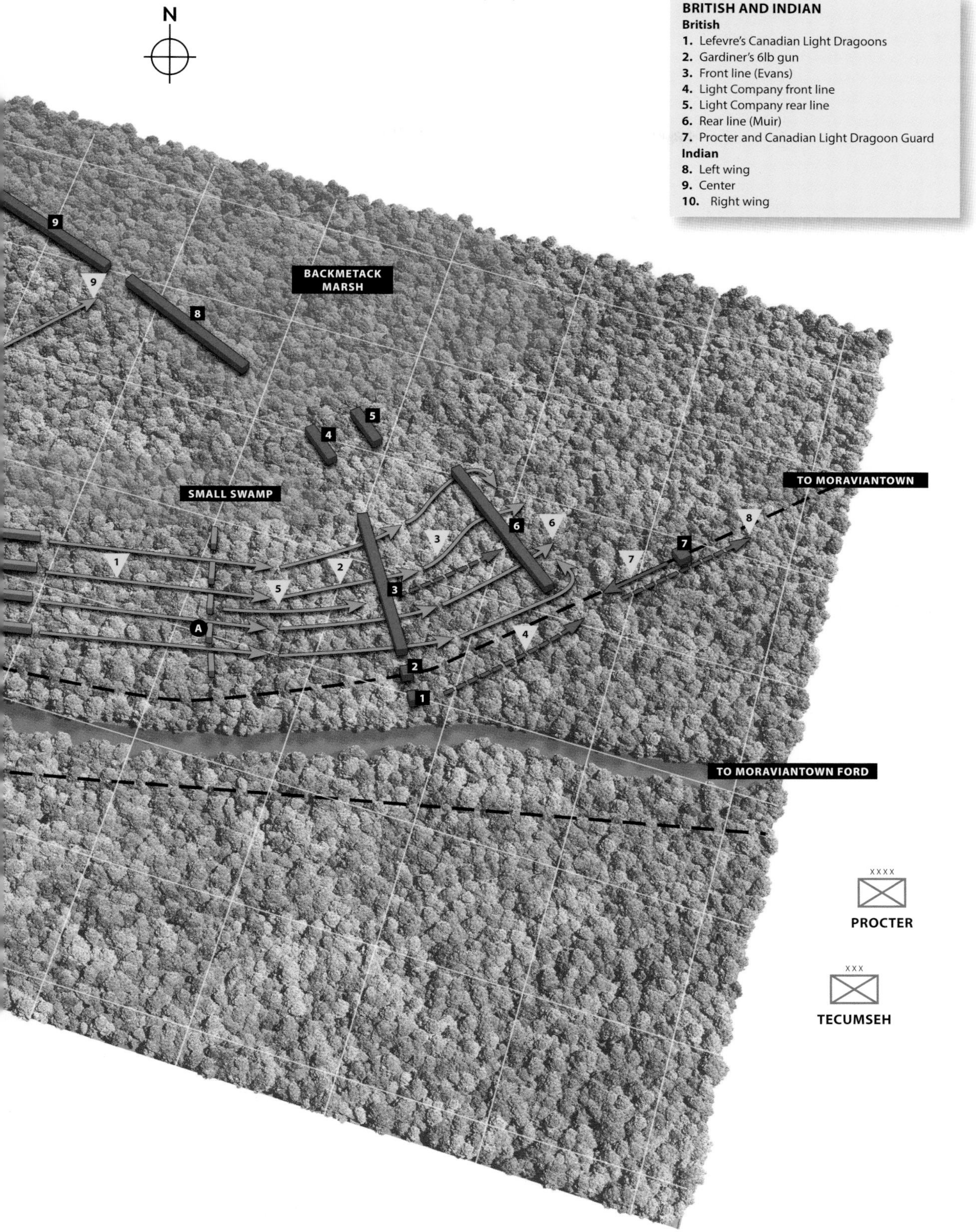

N

BRITISH AND INDIAN
British
1. Lefevre's Canadian Light Dragoons
2. Gardiner's 6lb gun
3. Front line (Evans)
4. Light Company front line
5. Light Company rear line
6. Rear line (Muir)
7. Procter and Canadian Light Dragoon Guard
Indian
8. Left wing
9. Center
10. Right wing

9

9

BACKMETACK MARSH

8

5

4

SMALL SWAMP

6

6

TO MORAVIANTOWN

3

1

2

8

5

7

7

A

3

4

2

1

TO MORAVIANTOWN FORD

XXXX

PROCTER

XXX

TECUMSEH

73

THE ADVANCE OF TECUMSEH'S INDIAN LEFT WING, OCTOBER 5, 4.20PM (PP. 74–75)

As the warriors in the Indian left wing waited in Backmetack Marsh for the signal to emerge and attack the Americans, Tecumseh, who led them, saw ahead a mounted man wearing an unusual hat and what appeared to be a white sash across his chest. Believing that it was the American commander, William Henry Harrison, the Shawnee went forward onto high ground beyond Backmetack Marsh to find a closer position from which to shoot him. Many warriors in the Indian left wing followed him forward.

A satisfied Tecumseh (**1**), who has fired his musket, and seen the figure in the distance hit by his ball, now wants to go further forward to claim the man's scalp. His close friend Shabbona (**2**), a Potawatomi commander, is to his left. The Potawatomi commander Mad Sturgeon (**3**), who led the Indians at Fort Dearborn, is firing at the mounted man whom Tecumseh has hit.

Behind are the Wyandot commander Split Log (**4**), brother of the famous chief Roundhead; and the adopted Shawnee Andrew Clark (**5**) who served as Tecumseh's interpreter. The Potawatomi Billy Caldwell (**6**) is firing at the figure. A Shawnee behind him (**7**) carries the standard of the Indian left wing. A Canadian ranger (**8**), sent by Colonel William Caldwell to learn whether Tecumseh wants the whole Indian left wing to advance from Backmetack Marsh, is hastening toward the Indian commander. Ahead in the distance, beyond the front and right of the advancing Kentuckians, is mortally wounded William Whitley (**9**), whom Tecumseh had mistaken for Harrison. Concealed by the woods beyond Whitley are Colonel Richard M. Johnson and the remainder of Whitley's Forlorn Hope (**10**), and Captain Jacob Stucker's advancing line of dismounted Kentucky riflemen (**11**).

4.15pm–4.30pm

When Harrison learned that James Johnson's horsemen had taken hundreds of British prisoners, he ordered forward to reinforce them Black Hoof's, Tarhe's, and the Conners' Indians; Paull's regulars; Trotter's regiment; and four companies of Donaldson's six-company regiment. By then, Richard Johnson's horsemen were ready to advance on the left toward Backmetack Marsh.

Johnson's goal was the Indian right flank; but the Kentucky commander had no way to know exactly where it was. He therefore had divided his force into two parts, which would together go forward on a front about 400 yards wide. On the right, where the horsemen were most likely to encounter stiff resistance, he and Whitley's 20-man Forlorn Hope would ride ahead of a 150-yard-wide line of 100 dismounted men in Captain Jacob Stucker's company. Behind them, captains James Coleman's and James Davidson's 180 horsemen would advance in 45 files, each four horsemen deep. About 100 yards to their left, Major David Thompson would lead the 180 men in captains William Rice's and Samuel Combs's companies in similar order.

About 4.15pm, the Kentuckians began walking their horses forward, around the thickets and through the underbrush toward Backmetack Marsh. Johnson's men moved slowly toward the Indian center, and Thompson's toward the Indian right wing. Three hundred yards ahead, the Indians were still waiting in the swamp for the signal from the 6lb gun.

After several minutes, the foremost men in the Forlorn Hope came in sight of the far right of Tecumseh's Indian left wing. Before dying of wounds suffered at the battle, Andrew Clark told Private Alfred Brunson and several other Americans what had happened then. Tecumseh, the Shawnee's interpreter said, had seen in the distance "a man on a fine horse, with a cocked hat on, and a wide wampum belt over his shoulder to which his powder-horn and bullet-pouch were hung, and being thus distinguished from every other man in the army, he supposed that it must be Harrison. He advanced from the line of the Indians to get a shot at him. In his advance he was followed by other Indians in the form of a harrow or triangle."

Tecumseh shot Whitley. Nine balls hit Emperor, who, unlike his rider, survived. Determined to get what he believed to be Harrison's scalp, Tecumseh then raced ahead, with warriors following him at a 45-degree angle from the original Indian line. A firefight followed with the rest of the Forlorn Hope.

The warriors in Tecumseh's Indian left wing fought under this standard. (Kentucky Historical Society, 1939.348.1)

Two balls hit Johnson. Return fire wounded Tecumseh. Stucker's dismounted men, and Davidson's and Coleman's arriving horsemen, then forced the Shawnee and his warriors back into the swamp.

The wounded Johnson, whose horse had been hit by three balls, led his men into the morass after them. "We charged into the swamp," recalled Knaggs, who was fighting with Stucker's company, "where several of our horses mired down." After Johnson received three more wounds, he was carried back to safety. Coleman, who assumed command, ordered the men to dismount. "The Indians," McAfee was told, "fired so hot that the companies had to dismount and fight from behind trees and logs in the Indian way."

Finally, recalled Knaggs, "An order was given to retire to the hard ground in our rear, which we did. We halted on the hard ground, and continued our fire." Still determined to get what he believed to be Harrison's scalp, the wounded Tecumseh led the Indians out of the swamp after them. "The Indians in front," Knaggs remembered, "believing that we were retreating, immediately advanced upon us, with Tecumseh at their head." An American ball killed the great Shawnee. "Repeated charges and repulses," McAfee recalled, then "took place on each side."

To keep warriors from the far left of the Indian left wing from flanking them, Coleman's men extended their line to the right. There, Davidson, who by now had three wounds, saw his 18-year-old brother-in-law David King fell a warrior.

Whitley carried this powder horn at the battle. The first part of the inscription reads: "William Whitley, I'm your horn The truth I love, a lie I scorn. Fill me with the best of powder, I'll make your rifle crack the louder."
(Photograph by Kenneth Orr)

As Coleman's Kentuckians moved ever further to their right, the fighting came within sight of the British light company. "A Kentucky riflemen," remembered John Richardson, "dismounted within a few yards of the spot where I stood." Three Indian musket balls then hit him. "Never," the young British ensign recalled, was fear so strongly depicted on the human countenance, and the man's hair (for he was uncovered) absolutely seemed to me to stand on end as he attempted to double a large fallen tree, in order to elude the weapons of his enemies." But a warrior soon reached the Kentuckian. "When within twelve or fifteen paces of the rifleman, he raised and threw his tomahawk, and with such precision and force, that it immediately opened the skull, and extended him motionless on the earth." Richardson then saw another Kentuckian "taking aim at one of the light company." "I fired," he recalled; "His rifle tumbled from his shoulder to the ground, and he sank over his horse's side."

4.30pm–4.55pm

Ahead of Thompson's men, the warriors in the Indian center and right wing had remained in Backmetack Marsh. At the edge of the swamp, the Kentucky commander had ordered his men to leave their horses. When they went forward on foot into the morass, the Indian right wing attacked their left flank. Thompson's outnumbered Kentuckians fell back from Oshawana's and Peckickee's Ojibwes, and Four Legs's and Naw Kaw's Winnebagos. "The Americans," remembered Lieutenant James Fraser of the Indian Department, "retreated until they came to an open place in the wood."

Naiwash's Ottawas and Winepagon's Ojibwes in the Indian center, then rushed forward to join the battle. Some attacked the right flank of Thompson's men, and others the left of Coleman's. Still others rushed into the gap between Thompson's and Coleman's embattled Kentuckians.

When Shelby learned that Coleman's men were under heavy pressure, he sent the remaining two companies of Donaldson's regiment forward. The 50-man companies of captains George Matthews and James Mason soon reached the warriors advancing between Thompson's and Coleman's men. In fierce fighting, the 100 Kentuckians halted them.

Shelby also sent Adair back with orders. Pogue's regiment was to occupy the ground from which Matthews's and Mason's companies had advanced. King was to bring Renick's and Taul's regiments forward to the positions previously occupied by Trotter's regiment and Donaldson's four companies.

By then, the reinforcements Harrison had sent to join James Johnson's horsemen had freed them for further operations. Johnson's second-in-command, Major DeVall Payne, led 200 of the Kentuckians toward Moraviantown in pursuit of Procter. Johnson himself led the other 280 toward the firing beyond the small swamp.

This colored lithograph from James Lewis's 1836 *Aboriginal Portfolio* reproduced his 1827 portrait of the Winnebago chief Four Legs. (Author's collection)

James Johnson's horsemen soon reached the British light company. The Kentuckians, remembered Richardson, were "rapidly upon us in every direction; so that the resistance the light company had hitherto opposed, was now utterly hopeless of any successful result." "After exchanging a few shots," remembered Byfield, "our men gave way. I was in the act of retreating, when one of our sergeants exclaimed, 'For God's sake, men, stand and fight.' I stood by him and fired one shot, but the line was broken and the men were retreating. I then made my escape farther into the wood."

After riding through the light company, James Johnson's horsemen reached the left flank of the Indians fighting Coleman's Kentuckians. There a warrior tried to stop Elliston. "An Indian," remembered Brown, "seized the bridle of his horse and attempted a blow with his tomahawk," but Elliston's saber killed him. Overwhelmed by Johnson's attack, the warriors in the unit the fallen Tecumseh had led fled back to the safety of their original positions in Backmetack Marsh.

As Coleman's men pursued the warriors in the Indian left wing, James Johnson's horsemen continued on toward the Indians battling Matthews's and Mason's Kentuckians. There, Wickliffe remembered, Winepagon's Ojibwes and Naiwash's Ottawas were making a "heavy and last charge."

Winepagon fell. Then the warriors learned that Johnson's approaching horsemen soon would cut off their line of retreat. Fifty-five minutes after the first fire in the battle, Wickliffe recalled, he heard "the Indian shout for retreat." "They gave," remembered Private William Greathouse, who was marching forward in Renick's regiment, "the loudest yells I ever heard from human beings and that ended the fight."

4.55pm–6.30pm

As the last of Naiwash's Ottawas tried to protect the Indian retreat to Backmetack Marsh, Desha, who had been posted at his line's center, rode up to its far right. Ahead, he remembered, Matthews's and Mason's companies

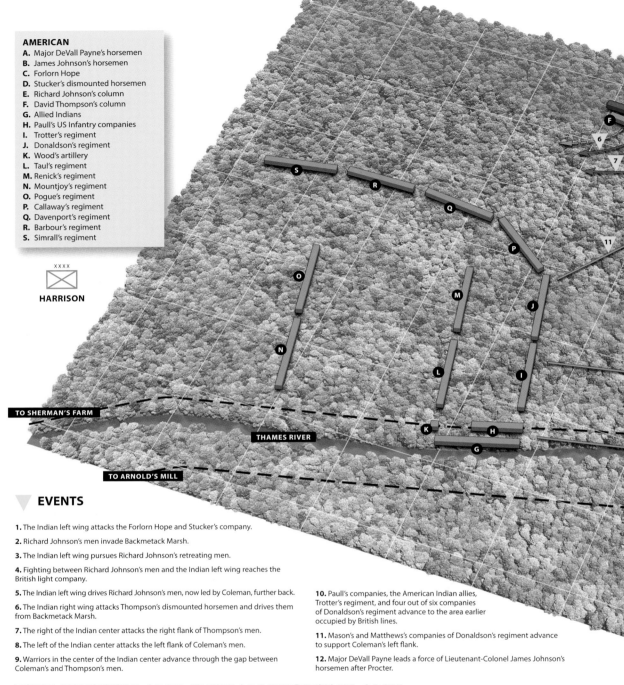

AMERICAN

A. Major DeVall Payne's horsemen
B. James Johnson's horsemen
C. Forlorn Hope
D. Stucker's dismounted horsemen
E. Richard Johnson's column
F. David Thompson's column
G. Allied Indians
H. Paull's US Infantry companies
I. Trotter's regiment
J. Donaldson's regiment
K. Wood's artillery
L. Taul's regiment
M. Renick's regiment
N. Mountjoy's regiment
O. Pogue's regiment
P. Callaway's regiment
Q. Davenport's regiment
R. Barbour's regiment
S. Simrall's regiment

xxxx

HARRISON

TO SHERMAN'S FARM

THAMES RIVER

TO ARNOLD'S MILL

▼ EVENTS

1. The Indian left wing attacks the Forlorn Hope and Stucker's company.

2. Richard Johnson's men invade Backmetack Marsh.

3. The Indian left wing pursues Richard Johnson's retreating men.

4. Fighting between Richard Johnson's men and the Indian left wing reaches the British light company.

5. The Indian left wing drives Richard Johnson's men, now led by Coleman, further back.

6. The Indian right wing attacks Thompson's dismounted horsemen and drives them from Backmetack Marsh.

7. The right of the Indian center attacks the right flank of Thompson's men.

8. The left of the Indian center attacks the left flank of Coleman's men.

9. Warriors in the center of the Indian center advance through the gap between Coleman's and Thompson's men.

10. Paull's companies, the American Indian allies, Trotter's regiment, and four out of six companies of Donaldson's regiment advance to the area earlier occupied by British lines.

11. Mason's and Matthews's companies of Donaldson's regiment advance to support Coleman's left flank.

12. Major DeVall Payne leads a force of Lieutenant-Colonel James Johnson's horsemen after Procter.

THE BRITISH AND INDIAN RIGHT FLANK, OCTOBER 5, 4.20PM–4.40PM

The successful charge of the Kentucky mounted riflemen on the American right was followed by a movement on the American left by another 480 mounted riflemen, who went forward into difficult, swampy terrain to find and engage the Indians at the far right of the British and Indian line. Led by Tecumseh, the Indians attacked the Kentuckians. Fierce fighting ensued. At the same time, the American commander sent forward a force of regulars, Kentucky militiamen, and allied Indians to defend the ground taken at the left of the British and Indian line, and to guard the British prisoners taken there.

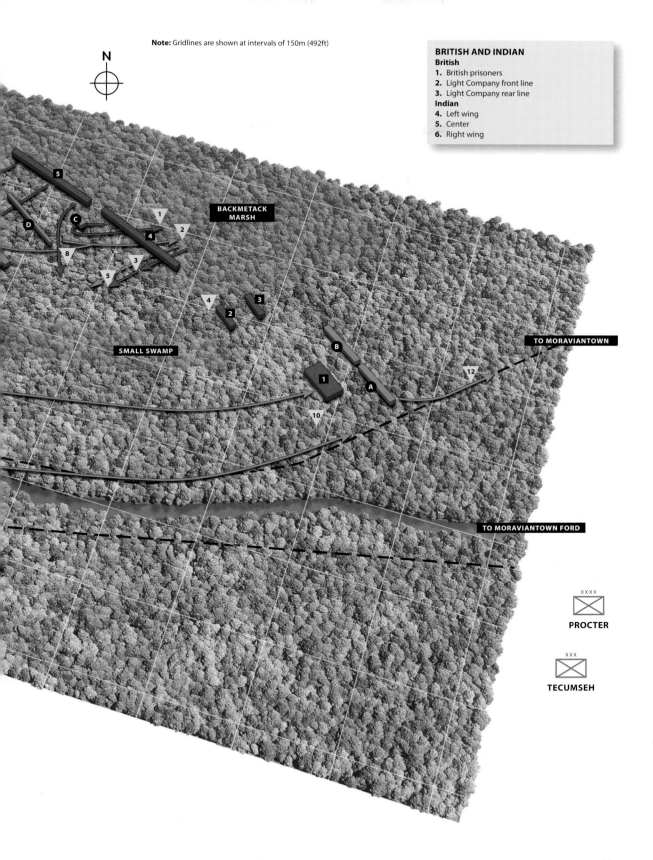

Note: Gridlines are shown at intervals of 150m (492ft)

N

BACKMETACK
MARSH

SMALL SWAMP

TO MORAVIANTOWN

TO MORAVIANTOWN FORD

PROCTER

TECUMSEH

THE INDIAN ATTACK ON MAJOR DAVID THOMPSON'S DISMOUNTED RIFLEMEN, OCTOBER 5, 4.30PM (PP. 82–83)

After dismounting and entering Backmetack Marsh, Major David Thompson's 180 men were attacked by about 520 warriors in the Indian right wing and center. The scene shows men in Captain William Rice's company, on Thompson's left, falling back from the onslaught.

This Kentuckian (**1**) has retreated along a path of high ground. Behind him, another Kentuckian is carrying a wounded friend (**2**). This Kentuckian (**3**) has shot a pursuing warrior (**4**), identifiable as a Winnebago by the snake skins hanging from his armbands.

Another Kentuckian is reloading his rifle (**5**). This Kentuckian (**6**), who has a hunting horn, is being told by Captain William Rice (**7**) to signal to Captain Samuel Combs's company, fighting to their right, that Rice's company is retreating. In the distance, the Winnebago chief Naw Kaw (**8**) is shouting to his warriors to advance. To his left, smoke reveals where warriors have opened fire on the Kentuckians (**9**). As some Winnebagos (**10**) begin wading toward the Kentuckians, others (**11**) are moving forward on high ground.

"were making a charge on the Indians to dislodge them from behind some logs from whence they were annoying them." He ordered his line to advance toward the Indians, Desha recalled, but they went forward "but a short distance when the firing ceased."

By then, the Ojibwes of Oshawana and Peckickee, and the Winnebagos of Four Legs and Naw Kaw, had driven Thompson's scattered Kentuckians back hundreds of yards. Some on the far right had reached James Allen's and Caldwell's brigades. "A number of men rushed into my line," recalled Desha.

Then, as Pogue's regiment arrived to support Desha's right, Ojibwes and Winnebagos pursuing Thompson's men reached the American left flank line. "There was some firing," remembered Desha. But the Indians found arrayed in the line 700 riflemen. "On their conceiving the formidable appearance of my men, they veered off to the left."

A few minutes later, Desha recalled, there again was gunfire "three or four hundred yards to the left." "Gov. Shelby," he remembered, "rode up and inquired loudly what men were engaged. I replied that I supposed the left of my division were pouring it in upon the enemy." When Shelby investigated, he learned that the fire was from Thompson's men. Ahead of the far left of Desha's line, they had halted the Ojibwes' and Winnebagos' advance.

"Governor Shelby," remembered McAfee, "rode down to the left of General Desha's division, and ordered the regiment of Colonel Simrall, which was posted on the extreme left, to march up on the right flank of the enemy, in aid of Major Thompson. But before this reinforcement could reach the scene of action, the Indians had given up the contest."

In their last effort, Peckickee fell about 5.15pm. "We then retreated to the Moravian village," Fraser remembered. But they could find no refuge there. "The American mounted men pursuing us," he recalled, "we were obliged to take to the woods again and night came on and that was the last we saw of them."

After fleeing through the trees with other men from the light company, Richardson finally reached the road to Moraviantown. But there he found a group of horsemen. "At their head," he remembered, was "a stout, elderly officer whom we subsequently knew to be Governor Shelby." The Kentucky governor, the British ensign recalled, "galloped forward and, brandishing his sword over his head, cried out with stentorian lungs 'Surrender. Surrender, it's no use resisting. All your people are taken, and you had better surrender.'"

As he was walking back to the battlefield to join the other prisoners, Richardson then saw ahead "a body of American Indians, about fifty in number, from one of whose tomahawks I apprehended the death blow … But my fear was without foundation. As I watched them more narrowly, I found that their countenances wore an expression of concern, and that, so far from seeking to injure us, they seemed rather to regret our fate."

Richardson was not alone in fearing the Indians more than the Americans. Byfield, who in the end reached Delaware safely, spent anxious hours alone with them. "We went forward until night came on, when the Indians halted and formed round me. They seemed to be holding a consultation. I supposed it was to decide how I should be disposed of. In this solitary place, and

This colored lithograph in McKenney and Hall's 1848 *History of the Indian Tribes of North America* reproduced an 1839 Charles Bird King portrait of the Winnebago chief Naw Kaw. (Author's collection)

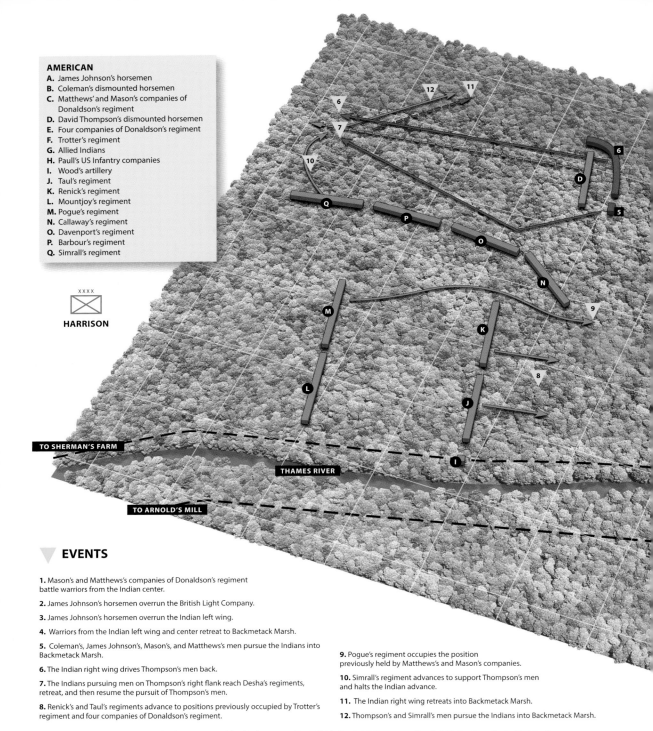

AMERICAN

A. James Johnson's horsemen
B. Coleman's dismounted horsemen
C. Matthews' and Mason's companies of Donaldson's regiment
D. David Thompson's dismounted horsemen
E. Four companies of Donaldson's regiment
F. Trotter's regiment
G. Allied Indians
H. Paull's US Infantry companies
I. Wood's artillery
J. Taul's regiment
K. Renick's regiment
L. Mountjoy's regiment
M. Pogue's regiment
N. Callaway's regiment
O. Davenport's regiment
P. Barbour's regiment
Q. Simrall's regiment

xxxx
HARRISON

TO SHERMAN'S FARM

THAMES RIVER

TO ARNOLD'S MILL

▼ EVENTS

1. Mason's and Matthews's companies of Donaldson's regiment battle warriors from the Indian center.

2. James Johnson's horsemen overrun the British Light Company.

3. James Johnson's horsemen overrun the Indian left wing.

4. Warriors from the Indian left wing and center retreat to Backmetack Marsh.

5. Coleman's, James Johnson's, Mason's, and Matthews's men pursue the Indians into Backmetack Marsh.

6. The Indian right wing drives Thompson's men back.

7. The Indians pursuing men on Thompson's right flank reach Desha's regiments, retreat, and then resume the pursuit of Thompson's men.

8. Renick's and Taul's regiments advance to positions previously occupied by Trotter's regiment and four companies of Donaldson's regiment.

9. Pogue's regiment occupies the position previously held by Matthews's and Mason's companies.

10. Simrall's regiment advances to support Thompson's men and halts the Indian advance.

11. The Indian right wing retreats into Backmetack Marsh.

12. Thompson's and Simrall's men pursue the Indians into Backmetack Marsh.

THE END OF THE BATTLE, OCTOBER 5, 4.40PM–6.30PM

The arrival of reinforcements allowed David Johnson's horsemen to resume active participation in the battle. As 200 began a 7-mile pursuit of Procter, the other 280 attacked and overran the remaining British company. They then assaulted the left flank of the Indians battling the Kentuckians. Fearing that the horsemen would cut off their line of retreat, the Indians ended their attack and fled into the swamp. The last Indians engaged in combat, at the far right of the Indian line, had driven the Kentuckians back hundreds of yards. They fled the field about an hour and a half after the battle commenced.

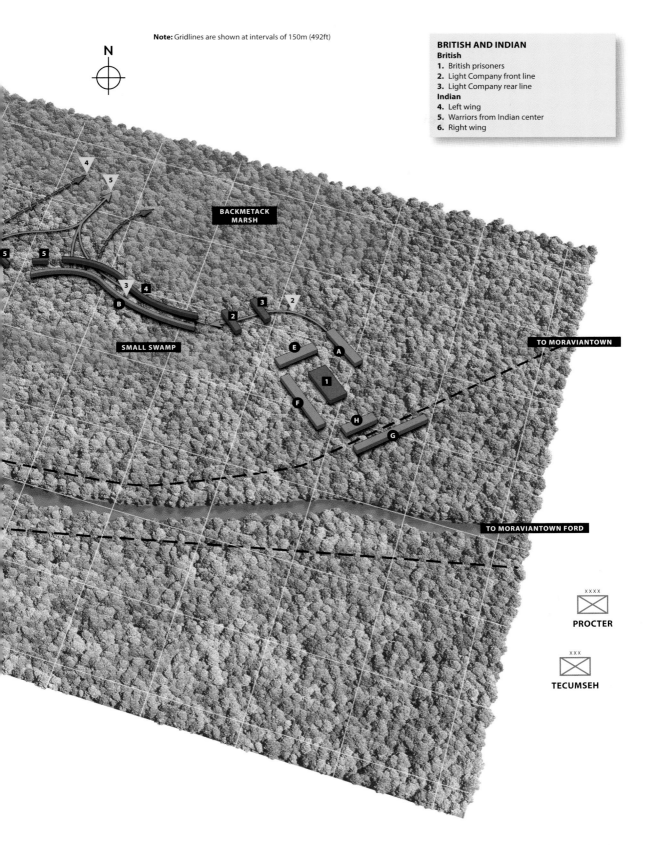

Note: Gridlines are shown at intervals of 150m (492ft)

N

BACKMETACK
MARSH

SMALL SWAMP

TO MORAVIANTOWN

TO MORAVIANTOWN FORD

XXXX
PROCTER

XXX
TECUMSEH

Mathew Jouett painted this portrait of Isaac Shelby in 1816. (Kentucky Historical Society, 1957.17.1)

This 41st Regiment of Foot drum was captured at Thames. (Kentucky Historical Society, 1909.22)

surrounded by savages whose cruelties I was somewhat acquainted with, I had but little hope, at the moment, of ever getting out of the woods."

After 6.30pm

When the last sunlight left the sky at 6.32pm, the exhausted Americans ended their search for fleeing enemies. After Payne's men, who had vainly pursued Procter for 7 miles beyond Moraviantown, returned with 50 more prisoners, they counted the day's gains and losses. Whitley and 14 other Americans were dead, and Berry, Richard Johnson, Davidson, and another 17 wounded.

Eighteen British soldiers were dead, and 25 wounded, the captured Warburton and Evans calculated. On October 5, Sympson remembered, the Americans took 472 British prisoners on the field, and another 78 elsewhere. In all, the British had lost 28 officers and 606 men from October 3 to 5.

The Indians, who left 33 bodies on the field, had about 40 dead, including Tecumseh, Winepagon, and Peckickee. Another 50 probably had been wounded. All night they made their way through the moonlit woods, searching for the camps where they had left their women and children. Naiwash and the Prophet ultimately persuaded about 125 warriors and their families to join the British at Delaware. The rest, as they tried to return to their distant homes, would risk starvation during winter journeys of hundreds of miles.

As the unhappy Indians made their way through the woods, the Americans and their prisoners ended the day in sleep. Two hundred Americans, and Payne's 50 prisoners, spent the night in Moraviantown, where McAfee was left in command. The rest camped on the battlefield.

The day, McAfee thought, had gone on long enough – and the fighting too. Thirty-three years before, his uncle William had fallen leading a company at Peckuwe. Richard and James Johnson's father had led a company there, and Elliston's father too. Shortly after 11.00pm, he ended his journal entry for the day. "I most fervently hope," McAfee wrote, "that a total separation has taken place between the British and Indians, and that peace will once more smile upon our northwestern frontiers, so long stained by the blood of innocent women and children."

At 3.00am, McAfee was awakened. Ensign James Cochran and six men had come out of the woods to surrender. The proud young officer, the Kentuckian added to his entry before returning to bed, was "a staunch friend of his country." "I felt much for him," McAfee concluded, "though I informed him of their cruel conduct to our prisoners, which he very much condemned."

At about the same time, Private Alfred Brunson recalled, the men on the battlefield were "all aroused and ordered to our arms at the loud outcry of a volunteer. He exclaimed: 'O Lord! O Lord! Indians! Indians!' We thought for a moment that they had attacked our lines. But it turned out that the man was asleep and dreaming."

AFTERMATH

On October 14, the chiefs who had fought with the British agreed to peace at a council in Detroit. Even Main Poc, whom Harrison called "the most inveterate of our enemies," had had enough. Three days later, the Kentuckians began returning home. Shelby's men found their horses waiting on the Marblehead Peninsula – as well as the Harrodsburg pig, which ended its days a pampered pet on Shelby's farm.

Many thought that Harrison now would be given command of all American forces in the war. But an angry Armstrong, who had been forced to approve Harrison's use of Shelby's militiamen, blocked any further promotion. On February 13, 1814, Harrison retired from military service.

Dickson continued to provide warriors for British operations hundreds of miles to the north and west of Detroit. There they defeated the Americans at the July 20, 1814 battle of Fort Shelby, July 26, 1814 battle of Mackinac Island, and July 21 and September 5, 1814 battles of the Rock River. But they could not recover Uppermost Canada and the Michigan Territory.

The British nonetheless announced in 1814 that they would discuss peace only if the Americans first agreed to accept a permanent border between American and Indian land. When the Americans refused, the confident British commenced a last effort to recover what Procter had lost.

The April 6, 1814 surrender and abdication of Napoleon had freed for operations in North America the army with which the Marquis (soon to become Duke) of Wellington had fought the French. On August 31, Prévost led 14,000 of Wellington's veterans across the border into New York. They would, he planned, march below Lake Ontario and Lake Erie to the Maumee Rapids, and sweep up to recover Detroit and Malden. But defeat at the September 11 battle of Plattsburgh ended the operation when Prévost's army was still 400 miles northeast of Lake Erie.

Led by McArthur, the Americans prevailed in the last operations in the Uppermost Canada area, small battles at Longwoods on March 4, 1814, and Malcolm's Mills on November 6, 1814. This 1868 George Hoffman portrait depicts McArthur, who would in 1838 be elected governor of Ohio. (Courtesy of Garth's Auctioneers and Appraisers, Inc.)

As Wellington's star had risen, Bathurst and Liverpool had increasingly turned to him for advice. Procter's invasion of Ohio would end badly, the great commander had predicted in a February 10, 1813 letter to Bathurst. Wellington now gave to Liverpool his view of the British position on peace negotiations. "You have not even cleared your own territory on the point of attack. You can get no territory. Indeed, the state of your military operations, however creditable, does not entitle you to demand any." The British abandoned their precondition for negotiations. The Americans agreed to return Uppermost Canada. Peace came in the Treaty of Ghent, which the US Senate approved on February 18, 1815.

American settlers then swarmed to the Northwest Frontier in hundreds of thousands. By 1820, the population of the states and territories north of the Ohio River was four times what it had been in 1810. In 1816, Indiana became a state; in 1818 Illinois; in 1837 Michigan. In 1848, what had been part of the Illinois Territory entered the Union as Wisconsin.

Britain turned its attention from Uppermost Canada to other remote areas of the world's greatest empire in its golden age. Although most of the captured men of the 41st chose to remain in America, the regiment was reconstructed for further service. In 1824, it would battle Burmese swordsmen; in 1842, Afghani tribesmen; and, in 1854, instead of Kentucky horsemen, cossacks in the Crimea.

There was trouble in 1832. When a Winnebago shaman saw in a vision that the British would again join the Indians, Black Hawk led his warriors against the Americans. But American soldiers and allied Indians quickly ended the Black Hawk War. It was, the British announced, an American affair of no interest to Britain.

Trouble returned in 1837. When unhappy Canadian settlers attempted to replace their government in the Upper Canada Rebellion, 93 Americans who joined them were captured and transported to penal servitude in Australia. But the United States did not intervene. It was an internal matter in Canada, said President Martin Van Buren, who had prosecuted Hull at his court martial, and Vice President Richard M. Johnson.

By then, the Indians on what had been the Northwest Frontier were only a minute fraction of the population. Few, if any, had more Indian than European ancestors. Many abandoned their tribal identities and blended into the larger population. Some remained on small tribal reserves. Others, like the Ohio Wyandots, traded their land for larger holdings farther west.

On July 21, 1843, the last Indian gunfire was heard in Ohio. Led by their chief, William Walker, Jr., the Wyandots were traveling down the Ohio River toward a new home in Missouri. When their riverboats passed Harrison's tomb in North Bend, they fired a volley to honor the great commander who had led them.

Three years after Thames, the black Methodist missionary John Stewart began a successful effort to convert the Ohio Wyandots. The Wyandots' 1824 church in Upper Sandusky is still used for Methodist services. (Photograph by Dale Benington)

For Walker, who had been one of Harrison's warriors, it brought back memories of men who had been old when he had been young. He remembered 72-year-old Tarhe, trotting to keep up with Johnson's horsemen. "When in his prime," Walker said, "he must have been a lithe, wiry man, capable of great endurance, as he marched at the rear of his warriors through the whole of General Harrison's campaign into Canada. He was an active participant in the Battle of the Thames."

By then, the days of Tarhe already had begun to fade into legend. For most who came after, they would all blur into a single scene. It would be somewhere in the woods between the Appalachian Mountains and the Great Lakes, with a cabin in the background, or perhaps the Ohio River. And there, constrained no longer by time or space, the frontiersmen and warriors would battle forever in an American Valhalla.

But for a while, men like Walker remained, able to provide from memory what imagination could not encompass. They had sad tales to tell aplenty. But their favorites were those that ended in laughter.

Hull's Americans, Reynolds remembered, killed a man from the 41st in a little fight with British soldiers and Main Poc's Potawatomis near the Canard River in 1812. Soon after, some of the dead man's friends saw his hair hanging from Main Poc's belt. Angry that he had failed to get an American scalp in the skirmish, the Potawatomi chief had "decided that any scalp was better than none." The scalped soldier's friends, who were angry too, "gave him a good thrashing for his pains."

Just before his company reached Detroit in 1813, Sholes liked to recall, their ship passed an abandoned house full of Indians. "The captain let slip an eighteen pounder into the front door. Indians poured out of the windows, some head and some feet foremost. As soon as they were on their feet they steered for the wood, their blankets streaming behind them. A more frightened set of devils never stood on two feet."

The photograph shows an 1871 reunion of River Raisin survivors in Monroe, Michigan. George Armstrong Custer, who would die five years later at Little Big Horn, addressed the gathering. Peter Navarre is at the far left of the front row. Custer is the third from the left of the standing figures. (Courtesy of the Monroe County Historical Museum)

There sometimes had been laughter even in Hell. Usher Parsons had been the surgeon on the *Lawrence*. During the battle of Lake Erie, he remembered, they brought the wounded down to his surgery "faster than I could attend to them." But Lieutenant John Yarnall's arrival with a scalp wound had been something special. A British shell had exploded a pile of white hammocks on the deck. The disintegrated fibers had "filled the air like down, and had settled like snow upon the blood-wet head and face of Yarnall. When he made his appearance below, his visage was ludicrous beyond description. His head appeared like that of a huge owl. The wounded roared with laughter, and cried out, 'The Devil himself has come among us.'"

By 1879, the few still around to tell such stories had lived on into a different world. Thomas Edison, who had been born 2 miles from the site of Fort Avery, had just invented the electric light bulb and phonograph. Twelve-year-old Wilbur Wright and his younger brother Orville were playing with paper airplanes at their house a mile from where Hull had assumed command in 1812. Rutherford Hayes, whose home was a mile from the site of Fort Stephenson, was the US President.

Born nine years after Thames, Hayes had survived five wounds to end the Civil War a major-general. By the standards of the Civil War, the battles of the Ohio Indian Wars had been only small engagements. But the measure of battles, Hayes knew, is the magnitude of their consequences – and the consequences of the battles from Point Pleasant to Thames already were beyond the power of anyone to reckon. Half of the 2.2 million men in the Union army had come from Kentucky, Ohio, Indiana, Illinois, Michigan, and Wisconsin. Ohio alone had provided 320,000, and also the great commanders Grant, Sherman, and Sheridan.

On an August 2, 1879 visit to an old soldiers' home in Washington, Hayes talked with William Gaines, a retired US Army sergeant. As an 11-year-old Kentucky boy, the old man told his distinguished visitor, he had gone on the Tippecanoe campaign to take care of his uncle's horses. He'd nearly lost his left thumb, Gaines added, showing Hayes a scar left by a warrior's tomahawk. Then, as a 13-year-old private in Owings's 24th Infantry, he had been at Fort Meigs, Fort Stephenson, and Thames. After hearing what it had been like at the sieges of the Ohio fortresses, Hayes finally asked the old veteran about Thames. "I recollect that day just as well as I do sitting in this chair," Gaines responded. "It was," he began, "their last battle."

Invited to visit the White House, William Gaines arrived in a new uniform he had been given. Unfortunately, the disappointed sergeant told Mrs Hayes, the trouser stripes had not been attached to show his rank. Mrs Hayes, who called for her sewing basket, then stitched on herself the stripes worn by Gaines in this photograph. (Courtesy of the Rutherford B. Hayes Presidential Center)

THE BATTLEFIELD TODAY

Many museums, parks, and monuments are at the sites of significant events during the campaign that ended at Thames. The Detroit Historical Museum, at 5401 Woodward Avenue, has exhibits on Fort Detroit. Mississinewa is commemorated by a marker near Marion, IN on County Road 308W 0.7 miles south of County Road W600N. The site of the two battles in Frenchtown is now River Raisin National Battlefield Park in Monroe, MI, where the Visitor's Center is at East Elm Avenue. The Monroe County Historical Museum at 126 Monroe Avenue has exhibits on Frenchtown. The Navarre-Anderson Trading Post is at 3775 North Custer Road. Fort Meigs has been reconstructed on its original site at 29100 West River Road, in Perrysburg, OH. The site of Fort Stephenson is now the Birchard Public Library, at 423 Croghan Street in Fremont, OH. The Perry's Victory and International Peace Memorial, a museum devoted to the battle of Lake Erie, is at 93 Delaware Avenue in Put-in-Bay, OH. The Erie Maritime Museum, the home of the US brig *Niagara*, is at 150 Front Street in Erie, PA.

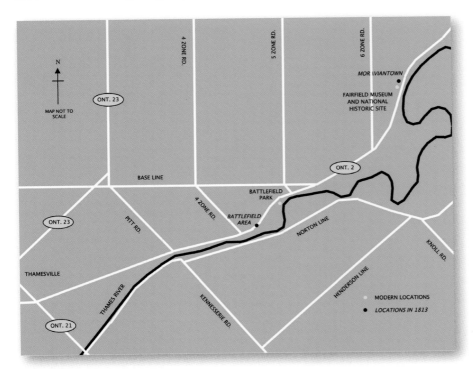

The battlefield today.
(Author's map)

The remains of Fort Malden can be seen at Fort Malden National Historic Site, at 100 Laird Avenue in Amherstburg, Ontario, where artifacts that belonged to Tecumseh and others who fought are displayed. The François Bâby House now is Windsor's Community Museum, at 254 Pitt Street West in Windsor, Ontario. Markers along Ontario Rte 2 commemorate sites from Drake's Farm to Moraviantown. The Chatham-Kent Museum, at 75 William Street North in Chatham, has exhibits on the campaign.

The battlefield, greatly altered since 1813, is southwest of the intersection of Longwoods Road (Ontario Rte 2) and 5 Zone Road, where a park contains many markers describing aspects of the battle. The Fairfield Museum and National Historic Site, at 14878 Longwoods Road, is at the site of Moraviantown.

Grouseland, where Harrison lived at the time he assumed command, now is a museum devoted to his life at 3 West Scott Street in Vincennes, IN. The William Whitley House State Historic Site is at 625 William Whitley Road, in Stanford, KY. William Conner's 1823 house is a museum at Conner Prairie Interactive History Park, at 13400 Allisonville Road in Fishers, IN. Charles Wickliffe's house is at 550 Bloomfield Road in Bardstown, KY. The Kentucky Military History Museum, at 125 East Main Street in Frankfort, displays many artifacts from the battle.

FURTHER READING

Antal, Sandy, *Wampum Denied: Procter's War of 1812*, McGill-Queen's Press, 1997

Brown, Samuel R., *An Authentic History of the Second War for Independence*, J.G. Hathaway, 1815

Brunson, Alfred, *A Western Pioneer*, Hitchcock and Walden, 1872

Coffin, William F., *1812, The War and its Moral: A Canadian Chronicle*, John Lovell, 1864

Edmunds, R. David, *The Potawatomis: Keepers of the Fire*, University of Oklahoma Press, 1978

——, "Forgotten Allies: The Loyal Shawnees and the War of 1812," in David C. Skaggs and Larry Nelson (eds.), *The Sixty Years' War for the Great Lakes, 1754–1814*, Michigan State University Press, 2001

Errington, E. Jane, "Reluctant Warriors: British North Americans and the War of 1812," in David C. Skaggs and Larry Nelson (eds.), *The Sixty Years' War for the Great Lakes, 1754–1814*, Michigan State University Press, 2001

Feltoe, Richard, *The Flames of War: The Fight for Upper Canada, July–December 1813*, Dundurn, 2013

Fredricksen, John C., "Kentucky at the Thames, 1813: A Rediscovered Narrative by William Greathouse," *Register of the Kentucky Historical Society*, Vol. 83, pp. 93–107, Frankfort, KY, 1985

Gilpin, Alec R., *The War of 1812 in the Old Northwest*, Michigan State University Press, 1958

Katcher, Philip, *The American War: 1812–14*, Men-at-Arms 226, Osprey Publishing, 1990

Kochan, James L., *The United States Army 1812–15*, Men-at-Arms 345, Osprey Publishing, 2000

Lossing, Benson J., *Pictorial Field-Book of the War of 1812*, Harper & Brothers, 1868

Nelson, Larry L., *Men of Patriotism, Courage and Enterprise: Fort Meigs and the War of 1812*, Heritage Books Inc., 1985

Olmstead, Earl P., *Blackcoats Among the Delaware: David Zeisberger on the Ohio Frontier*, Kent State University Press, 1991

Richardson, John, *Richardson's War of 1812*, Toronto, Historical Publishing Co., 1902

Skaggs, David C., *William Henry Harrison and the Conquest of the Ohio Country: Frontier Fighting in the War of 1812*, Johns Hopkins University Press, 2014

Sholes, Stanton, "Narrative of the Northwest Campaign of 1813," *Mississippi Valley Historical Review*, Vol. 15, pp. 522–50, Urbana, IL, 1929

Sugden, John, *Tecumseh's Last Stand*, University of Oklahoma Press, 1985

——, *Tecumseh: A Life*, Henry Holt & Co., 1997

Tanner, Helen H., *Atlas of Great Lakes Indian History*, University of Oklahoma Press, 1987

Wickliffe, Charles A., "Tecumseh and the Battle of the Thames," *Register of the Kentucky Historical Society*, Vol. 60, pp. 45–49, Frankfort, KY, 1962

Young, Bennett H., *The Battle of the Thames*, Filson Club Publications, 1903

INDEX